What Can We Do About Church Dropouts?

Creative Leadership Series

What Can We Do About Church Dropouts?

C. Kirk Hadaway

Creative Leadership Series
Lyle E. Schaller, Editor

Abingdon Press/Nashville

WHAT CAN WE DO ABOUT CHURCH DROPOUTS?

Copyright © 1990 by Abingdon Press

This book is printed on acid-free paper.

Library of Congress Cataloging-in-Publication Data

Hadaway, C. Kirk.
  What can we do about church dropouts? / C. Kirk Hadaway.
    p.   cm.—(Creative leadership series)
  Includes bibliographical references.
  ISBN 0-687-44605-8 (alk. paper)
  1. Ex-church members—United States. 2. Pastoral theology—United States. 3. Evangelistic work—United States. I. Title.
II. Series.
BV4013.H33 1990
253—dc20
                                      90-34749
                                       CIP

MANUFACTURED IN THE UNITED STATES OF AMERICA

Foreword

"Why should we try to win more new members when we can't keep the ones we already have?" challenged a belligerent member. "We're losing people out the back door as fast as we bring them in the front door. I believe we need to close that back door first and then look at how we can bring more people in the front door."

* * * * *

"We're experiencing a normal, natural, and predictable pattern," explained the pastor to a group of leaders who were troubled by the growing number of members who were classified as inactive or who had simply disappeared. "This is a normal consequence of rapid growth. The faster the rate of growth, the larger the number of people who eventually conclude that this is not the right church for them and so they move on. Don't worry about it. During the past five years we've received more than four hundred new members. That number compares to fewer than a hundred new members who were received by this congregation in the previous five-year period. Rapid growth causes a higher drop out rate. There's not much we can do about that, so let's concentrate on enlisting more new members next year."

* * * * *

"My advice to you is to develop a strategy for reaching the unchurched," urged a denominational representative after spending two days with the leaders of a seventy-two-year-old suburban congregation that had experienced a 50 percent decline in worship attendance during the past decade. "Studies conducted in this metropolitan area reveal that more than one-half of the residents are unchurched. The fields are ripe for the harvest. Identify your strengths, your resources, and your assets. Build on these as you decide which slice of the unchurched population you want to win to Christ. You have a fine building at a good location, and a cadre of devoted members. I'm sure you can double in size within a decade if you formulate and implement a strategy for reaching the unchurched."

"I know we have a lot of unchurched people in this community," agreed the discouraged pastor, "but I think you oversimplify the situation. The people around here can be divided into two groups: those who want to go to church and those who don't. The people in the first group already have found a church home for themselves, and those in the second group are unchurched because they feel that the church is irrelevant to their needs. I haven't seen the surveys you refer to, but I'm convinced that trying to convert the unchurched is a hopeless task in this community."

* * * * *

"If you ask me, dropping out of church is a normal and predictable part of youthful rebellion against parental control, and there's nothing we can do about it," advised the fifty-three-year-old father of three children—ages 27,

23, and 19—as he met with other members of the Evangelism Committee at First Church. "All three of our kids dropped out of church when they left home, and neither of the younger two go to church today. Two years ago our oldest married a lovely young woman who has always been an active church member, and now he is back in church. Some of you want us to make retention of our young people a high priority, but I don't think that can be done. Let's concentrate on winning new adult members and not worry about teenagers dropping out."

"Did your new daughter-in-law drop out of church when she was a teenager?" inquired a member of the committee.

"No, as far as I know, she didn't," conceded the father, "but she's an exception, not the rule."

* * * * *

These four brief conversations represent several of the most widely shared stereotypes of people who have dropped out of church and those who sometimes are described as "the unchurched." Each one of these four sets of comments contains a grain of truth. Each also contains some of the more popular misconceptions about dropouts, the unchurched, and strategies to reach them.

Each of these four conversations represents a segment of the audience to which this book is directed. Why do people drop out? How can a church close the famous wide-open "back door"? Must churches that are experiencing a rapid influx of new members accept as inevitable that many of these new members soon will depart? Is it possible to distinguish among the varying needs of new members and thus reduce the size of the exodus?

It is true that a large proportion of the adult population does not actively participate in the life of any worshiping community. Can any one congregation develop and implement a strategy to reach these unchurched adults? Would it be more realistic and practical first to identify which portion of the unchurched population a congregation has the resources to reach and serve? Or is it true that once adults have decided to stay away from church they cannot be persuaded to return? What are the characteristics of the people who constitute the unchurched population? Which slice of this population can your congregation seek to reach?

Is the disappearance from church of older teenagers and young adults an inevitable fact of life that no one can change, or can a congregation develop and implement a strategy to improve the retention of younger members? If so, what are the key components of such a strategy? Should the emphasis be placed on reaching those in their mid to late twenties who may be ready to return to church? How influential is marriage in this sequence?

These are among the scores of questions answered in this exceptionally lucid and helpful study of dropouts. All too often books of this nature are long on diagnosis and description and short on prescription. In this benchmark study, Kirk Hadaway provides us with the definitive descriptions of today's dropouts and dozens of practical, sensible, helpful, and relevant suggestions for specific courses of action.

Are you concerned about the millions of people of all ages who drop out of church every year? If you are, read this book! This book will enable you to understand the many facets of the "drop out problem," to review alternative courses of action as you seek to reduce the number who drop out of your church each year, and to develop a specific strategy to reach and win those who are now unchurched.

Lyle E. Schaller
Yokefellow Institute
Richmond, Indiana

Contents

Preface

This is a book about church dropouts—persons who drifted away, who fled, or who feel that they have been pushed out. They are a large population, and one which continues to expand. Who are these people, why have they left the church, and what can we do about them? Some want to return and would welcome expressions of love and understanding from church members, but most have no interest in returning because they feel that their reasons for staying away are valid.

This book is not primarily about those who have never identified with any church. This group of Second Generation Nones or "hard-core unchurched" will be considered, but the primary focus is on those who have been baptized, have made a profession of faith, or have grown up with a commitment to some church and subsequently have dropped out.

Church professionals and lay leaders realize that the church has a large "back door." It is so large, in fact, that real growth is difficult for most congregations. Membership rolls may increase, but Sunday school and worship attendance remain static or even decline. What prevents real growth is a steady stream of dropouts—a stream which runs particularly strong among the youth and young adults of North America.

Most dropouts retain a nominal church identity, but their attendance, commitment, and giving is far too sporadic to be noticed—much less to be a significant contribution to the vitality of the "church of their choice."

The purpose of this book is to describe and prescribe. The description will break stereotypes of dropouts. The great variety in this population will become clear as pictures of dropout types are drawn. The prescriptive part of the book is the practical, "what can we do about dropouts" component. This section also is divided into two parts. Covered first is the topic of how to reach the dropouts by using innovative and more traditional approaches to ministry. Considered second is the issue of prevention. The easiest dropout to reach is one who never left. My focus is on how our churches can "slow the flow" and keep members from drifting away, from fleeing, or from accidentally (or purposefully) being pushed into the unchurched pool.

This book had its origin in a series of studies that Wade Clark Roof and I conducted on patterns of denominational switching. In 1976 we began to investigate the characteristics of persons who switch denominations versus those who do not, the impact of switching on denominational growth and decline, and the factors that seem to influence people to switch. Although most persons who change their religious identity switch from one denomination to another, we found that there is an expanding group of Americans who drop out of religion altogether. These individuals were called the *Nones*, and they have been described in several articles written primarily for a social science audience.[1]

Several years ago I was asked to conduct a comprehensive study of one type of *None*—persons who were reared with a church identification but who rejected it later in life. This study was published in *Falling From the Faith: Causes and Consequences of Religious Apostasy*.[2] In evaluating the determinants of apostasy, or dropping out, it became clear that certain factors that were associated with dropping out seemed contradictory. Further research suggested that this was due to the existence of relatively distinct types of dropouts.

Using survey data from the National Opinion Research Center, it was possible to cluster dropouts into five groups, and to describe these groups in terms of their background social characteristics, their attitudes, and their reported behavior. The results of this research have appeared in several forms—most recently as an article in the *Journal for the Scientific Study of Religion.*[3]

This book became a vehicle for expanding my description of dropout types and for adding the "what to do about it" component, which was inappropriate for a social science journal. It begins with an introductory chapter on the nature of religious belonging in America. This chapter looks at the socio-cultural meaning of religious identification and how patterns of affiliation and disaffiliation have changed in the American setting. Particular attention is given to the past several decades of religious history, which have seen a rapid expansion of the dropout population and serious membership declines in many denominations.

The second chapter describes three types of Mental Members—persons who still identify with a church or denomination but who rarely, if ever, attend religious services. Although these individuals have not dropped out in the same sense as those who have totally rejected a church identity, Mental Members—who constitute the largest group of unchurched Americans—have dropped out of the church in terms of behavior. Mental Members are divided into three groups: (1) the Estranged; (2) the Indifferent; and (3) the Nominals. Each group is described in terms of their social characteristics and their reasons for minimal involvement in the church.

Chapter 3 looks at approaches that can be taken to

reclaim the two largest sub-types of Mental Members and also at ways to "slow the flow" of church members into their ranks. It is the first of several chapters that focus on practical applications to the information given in the more descriptive chapters.

Chapter 4 describes four groups of true dropouts—those who had a church identity in their youth but who rejected that identity later in life. All of the groups described in this chapter are comprised of young dropouts. (The one group of older dropouts is described in chapter 7.)

Chapters 5 and 6 look at younger dropouts in terms of what can be done. Chapter 5 deals with how they can be reclaimed by churches that are interested in reaching truly unchurched persons rather than in growing through transfers from other congregations. Chapter 6 covers methods of dropout prevention.

Chapter 7 considers two groups of *Nones* that are extremely resistant to the witness of churches. The first is the only group of older dropouts, the Irreligious Traditionalists. These are dropouts who are in their forties, fifties, and sixties, and who combine traditional, conservative values with an extreme level of irreligiosity. The second half of chapter 7 deals with Second Generation Nones—persons who had no religious identity when growing up and still have no religious identity. They are not dropouts, but they are hard-core unchurched persons; and they are described here for this reason.

The final chapter of the book is titled "To Reach the Unreachable. . . ." Its focus is on how to approach Irreligious Traditionalists and Second Generation Nones with a gospel message. Doing so may be difficult and frustrating, but churches in America cannot afford to write off this segment of the population. For churches who want to reach the lost, these people are lost, and many are proud of it. There is no danger of "sheep stealing" here.

Categorizing persons as dropout types should not imply that we should treat people as labels. We may "type" persons we meet, but we should resist making the assumption that because someone has certain characteristics of one dropout group he or she automatically has all of the other characteristics. People are complex, and in our face-to-face dealings with dropouts we should treat them as human beings with needs and feelings, not as categories. The categories are constructed to help us better understand those who have left the church and therefore to know how to relate to them in a more intelligent and redemptive manner.

Who should read this book? Anyone who is concerned about the unchurched, about dropouts, about those who have never experienced the church, about the disaffection of so many young adults from the church, or about the membership declines in so many churches and denominations. That should cover just about everyone, except for the dropouts themselves. To narrow the audience somewhat, this book has been written for pastors, ministers of missions and evangelism, deacons, evangelism committee members, membership committee members, denominational program leaders and consultants, and seminary faculty and students. In other words, it has been written for those who are in the position to actually use this material because it is intended to be used rather than simply to help interested readers understand the nature of dropouts in North America.

Exactly how the book can be used will become clearer in the prescriptive "what do we do about it" chapters. But in order to set the stage for those who do not wish to thumb ahead, it can be said that the idea is to help church leaders initiate and tailor specific strategies for reaching and reclaiming dropouts and for restricting the flow of church members (and the children of members) into the dropout population. Until we become intentional about this process we can only look forward to the legacy of the past twenty-five years: a slow attrition of members from mainline churches and the illusion of church growth through the "circulation of the saints."

I express special thanks to Lyle Schaller and Penny Long Marler for their helpful comments and suggestions on earlier drafts. Although some suggestions seemed painful at the time, they made this a better book.

I

Religious Belonging in America

"I'm a dropout. I once was an active United Methodist, but now I no longer attend church. In fact, I don't even call myself a Methodist anymore. . . . You want to know my religious preference? Well, I guess I don't have one—I'm not anything."

Most of us can form a mental picture of this former United Methodist—now nothing. The picture may be of a neighbor, a friend, or a family member. We all know people who are outside the church—whether they dropped out or never dropped in. There are millions of them in America. Each has a story and all have reasons why they have no use or no time for the church.

There is no single type of "unchurched" person, and, in fact, considerable confusion exists over who is unchurched and who is not. The Gallup Organization has defined the unchurched as persons who are not church members or persons who are church members who have not attended church in the past six months (weddings and funerals don't count). According to this definition, 43 percent of the United States adult population was unchurched in 1988—over 78 million adults.[1] This rather broad definition of the unchurched fosters the kind of numbers that impress audiences at evangelism conferences. People shake their heads at the "lostness" of America and, one hopes, commit themselves to doing something about it rather than decide that the task is too big and therefore futile.

An even larger number can be obtained when efforts are made to estimate the number of "unsaved" people in the United States. The Home Mission Board of the Southern Baptist Convention, for instance, estimates that there are 167 million "lost people" in the United States. The proportion of lost people varies from region to region. The Home Mission Board determined that 52.8 percent of the population of the east-south-central region of the United States is "lost," and, in contrast, 81.5 percent of the pacific region is "lost."[2]

In the final reckoning we all may be either sheep or goats—saved or lost—but being "churched" is a matter of degree. Involvement in the church can range from a "pillar of the church"—someone who is there every time the doors open, chairs several committees, serves on the board of deacons, visits prospects, and teaches Sunday school—to the town heathen—someone who never has been to church, claims to have no religion, and intends never to darken the door of a church (not even for his own funeral). Somewhere between these two extremes an arbitrary line can be drawn to separate the "churched" from the "unchurched." Just how close this line is to the overworked deacon or to the "hard-core heathen" is a matter for debate.

Rather than drawing a single dividing line between those in the church and those outside the church, this book draws several lines. All persons are not equally unchurched, and so they will not be treated the same. Some unchurched persons are Mental Members who belong to a church but rarely attend. Other unchurched persons once belonged but have dropped out, and still others have never belonged. All three groups of the unchurched are described, but special attention is given to those who once were part of the church but no longer identify with any church or denomination. In previous studies such persons have been called apostates, disaffiliates, religious leave-takers, defectors, and even

18

back-sliders. The term used here, however, will be *dropouts.* It may lack a certain degree of precision, but it is familiar and does not have the theological baggage of the term *apostate.*

Is America a Religious Nation?

Many motives exist for church membership and church attendance other than the need to worship God. People attend church to meet new friends, to gain business contacts, to win community acceptance, to expose their children to moral values, to find dates, and many other reasons. Similarly, the reasons for claiming a religious identity—for saying "I am a Presbyterian"—go far beyond the objective reality of belonging to or attending a Presbyterian church. Around 92 percent of Americans have a religious preference.[3] That is, when asked, people say, "I am a Baptist" (a Buddhist, a Jehovah's Witness, or something else). It may seem odd, however, that a large number of those who express such an identity are not members of any congregation and may rarely attend religious services at "the church of their choice." In fact, at least 40 percent more people claim to be Methodists, or Lutherans, or Episcopalians, or Presbyterians than actually are reported as members by those denominational families.

To have a religious identity is normal in American society. Despite the presence of relatively few social pressures to attend church or to have a religious identity, the majority of Americans do attend religious services at least a few times during the year, and almost all Americans have a religious preference.[4]

Those who bemoan the "lostness of America" may use illustrations of young adults who have never seen the Bible or heard of Jesus, but real-life examples of such persons are very hard to find in this society. Only 3 percent of Americans say that they were raised with no religion, and almost 60 percent of these *Nones* convert to some religion by the time that they are interviewed in national surveys.[5] Of the approximately 1.2 percent of Americans who remain *Nones* into adulthood, the majority are well educated and certainly have had some exposure to Christianity. For a nation in which true freedom of religion exists, a remarkably large percentage of Americans choose to be religious—if only in a superficial way.

Religious denominations in America are part of the dominant culture. The values they teach are as much American values as they are Christian or Jewish. When people say that they are Church of Christ or Episcopalian, they are not necessarily saying that they are committed church members. Rather, they may be saying that they affirm and identify with what those particular religious groups symbolize. Such people are pro-God in the same way that they are pro-American, and the two "pros" are rather tightly intertwined. In this society, to be a "good American" one must be a "good Christian," and to be a "good Christian" one should be a "patriotic American."

Frequent church attendance, although viewed as a "good thing," is also a very optional thing. In other words, it's fine never to attend church as long as you say that you are *something,* and that you would like to go to church more if you only had the time and could find the right church, and so on.

There are, of course, many intensely religious people in America, and their numbers have not dwindled in recent years. In fact, just as the percentage of persons who say that they are *Nones* has increased somewhat since the early 1970s, the percentage of persons who say that they attend church several times a week also has been on the rise until very recently.[6] The United States is a very religious nation and, at the same time, a very secular nation; and it can appear as either, depending on the statistics that are used.

In this religious environment, the person who drops a church identity is something of a peculiarity. Dropouts have moved beyond the socially accepted life-style of intermittent church attendance by taking the socially disapproved step of rejecting a religious label altogether. Even though the actual costs of this rejection are few, the fact that a nominal religious identity can be maintained with so few personal demands makes the decision to reject the identity puzzling—and often upsetting to friends and family. It is much simpler to remain *something* in this society. The reason many people have chosen a more difficult path is one of the questions addressed in this book.

Patterns of Apostasy

Many cultural myths exist in this society. George Washington did not literally cut down a cherry tree and confess, "I cannot tell a lie." Davy Crockett did not patch the crack in the Liberty Bell, and Wyatt Earp was as much a villain as he was a hero. Another American myth is the religious nature of our forebears. As everyone knows, the Pilgrims and other persecuted religious minorities fled to America to find religious freedom. They formed tightly knit, intensely religious communities, carved turkeys, burned witches, sang psalms, killed Indians, and eventually threw out the British. Since these idyllic days, Americans have become steadily less religious and God-fearing.

Students of American history have learned that the Pilgrim era was very short-lived. Colonists rapidly dispersed westward, usually leaving the church behind. Churches eventually were established in new villages, but membership requirements were so strict that most of the population were excluded. It may come as a surprise to some that by the time of the American Revolution, the percentage of the population who were church members was not 80 percent, or even 50 percent. In fact, the most reliable estimates put the number at less than 10 percent of the population.[7] People believed in God, but they were not generally church members. Perhaps even more disturbing is that many of the intellectual leaders of the day were not Christians. Thomas

21

Jefferson, Thomas Paine, Ethan Allen, John Adams, and others were essentially deists, followers of "rational religion," who saw Jesus as merely one of many religious teachers.

Revolutionary America, with a population of 3.9 million and only 3,223 churches, was an unchurched mission field.[8] It was not to remain so for long, however. A series of massive religious revivals swept the eastern seaboard and eventually reached the frontier south and midwest. During this era, Methodist, Baptist, and Presbyterian churches were established in huge numbers and eventually displaced the Episcopal Church and the Congregationalist Church as the dominant religious denominations in America.

The net result of the Great Awakenings and the churches that were spawned was a dramatic change in the religious landscape. The proportion of Americans who were church members rose from between 7 and 10 percent in 1776 to 34 percent by 1850. Historians estimate that Protestant membership increased tenfold between 1800 and 1850.[9] But the growth did not stop there. Membership reached 50 percent by the turn of the century and eventually rose to its highest levels of over 70 percent in the 1940s and 1950s.[10] Today approximately 61 percent of adult Americans say that they are church members, according to national public opinion polls.[11]

Rather than beginning as a very religious nation, the United States began as a very irreligious nation—at least as measured by church membership—and rather than becoming less religious since the eighteenth century, the United States has become more religious.

As the proportion of Americans who were church members rose, the percentage who indicated a religious preference rose even more. Unfortunately, accurate survey data is not available to document this rise. Still, we know that by the mid 1950s approximately 98 percent of Americans had a religious preference. This figure has not been that high since. The proportion of Americans who say that they have no religious preference rose from 2 percent in the mid 1950s to 3 percent in the mid 1960s before taking a big jump to 5 percent in 1972 and to 7.6 percent in 1975.[12] Since then the level has dropped slightly, stabilizing at just over 7 percent. In 1988 and 1989, the percentage who said that they were *Nones* climbed to 8 percent in several national polls.[13] It is too early to tell, however, whether or not this rise is the beginning of a trend.

Religious participation rose and fell in much the same manner as religious identification. Gallup poll data on the percentage of Americans who report attending religious services in the past week rose from 41 percent in 1939 (when the question was first asked) to a high of 49 percent in 1958 before dropping to 43 percent in 1967 and to 40 percent in 1972. At this point the figure essentially stabilized with minor yearly fluctuations.

Trend data on "dropping out of religion" are much harder to find than is information on church membership, religious identification, and church attendance. However, the limited data which are available clearly show that from 1960 to 1978 there were increases in the percentage of the population that dropped out of religion. Since 1978 these increases have stabilized and even may have reversed among some age groups.[14]

Religious change in this country seems to occur primarily through new generations or what sociologists call *age cohorts*. The religious orientation of a cohort of Americans is "set" sometime during their late teens and early twenties and tends to remain relatively constant over time. The orientation may be altered to a small extent as members react to changes in the culture. In general, however, cultural changes are reflected more in the religious orientation of each new age cohort that "comes on line" than they are in the religious orientation of older cohorts.

For instance, in 1960, 2.6 percent of persons age twenty to twenty-nine (the age cohort born from 1931 to 1940) had no religion. Ten years later, in 1970, the proportion of this *same generation* with no religion had increased to 3.5 percent. In the same year, the percentage of the *next generation* (those born from 1941 to 1950) with no religion was much higher: 7.1 percent. The same thing happened in 1980. Those born from 1941 to 1950 had 8.8 percent *Nones* among their ranks (up from 7.1 percent), but the new generation (those born from 1951 to 1960) had 12.6 percent *Nones*.[15]

What all of this means is that older age cohorts (persons born in the 1910–1930 era) have a higher average level of church participation and a lower proportion of *Nones* than any generation that has come *before or since*. Older age cohorts have *always* had high levels of participation—even when they were young. The data also imply that the huge baby boom generation will likely *never* reach the levels of religious activity present in older generations. More recent statistics (from 1984 and 1988) suggest that baby boomers are beginning to moderate their rejection of the church, but no massive return to the church is apparent nor can be anticipated.

The sign for a new religious revival or spiritual awakening which could return the United States to high levels of religious participation is more likely to be seen among high school students and young adults than among the baby boomers. Unfortunately, no such sign is apparent, but it is clear that the pattern of increasing disaffiliation seen from 1960 to 1980 has abated somewhat. Poll data for the mid and late 1980s indicate that the trend continues for new age cohorts to have a higher percentage of *Nones* than the age groups that came before them—although not to the extent of previous years. This abatement, coupled with the return to the church of some baby boomers (and those born just prior to the baby boom era), has resulted in a stabilization in the proportion of *Nones* in America—but certainly there is no religious revival.

Who is Being Hurt?

The increasing proportion of dropouts, decreasing church participation, and the erosion in the proportion of adults who retain church membership have had dramatic effects on mainline Protestant denominations in America. Membership decline, which began among some groups in the mid 1960s and spread to all liberal mainline denominations by the early 1970s, became the rule and continues today. As Clark Roof and Bill McKinney noted in 1985, "The losses in the 1970–80 period were staggering: the United Presbyterian Church, down 19 percent; Disciples, 17 percent; the Episcopalians, 15 percent; United Church of Christ, 11 percent; and The United Methodist Church, more than 9 percent."[16] As they also note, the declines were quite sudden and occurred at nearly the same time.

For some reason, authors who describe the liberal losses tend to contrast the losses with a "conservative resurgence." This sounds reasonable; but, like the new social conservatism which supposedly hit the American public in the 1980s, it simply did not happen.[17] The conservative denominations which are used to illustrate the conservative resurgence were growing most rapidly at the same time that the liberal denominations were growing most rapidly, and the growth of the conservatives tended to exceed the growth of the liberals even then (in the 1940s and 1950s).[18]

Surprisingly, conservative denominations were also hurt by the religious changes of the 1970s. They saw their growth rates plummet, but the rates did not dip low enough to actually result in decline. The Assemblies of God grew 25.6 percent from 1950 to 1955, but from 1975 to 1980 their growth rate slipped to 9.3 percent. Dramatic drops in growth rates were also experienced by the Church of God (Anderson, Indiana) and the Church of the Nazarene, to name just a few. In the Southern Baptist Convention, which is often used as a key example of the "conservative resurgence," membership gain was a robust 4.7 percent during the year 1950. By 1965, the annual rate of growth had dropped to 1.6 percent, and by 1978 it reached a low of .9 percent. Similarly, in the late 1950s and even the early 1960s, Southern Baptists experienced net gains in churches in the order of three to four hundred. By 1972, the net gain had dropped to only twenty-five churches.[19]

The resurgence myth was supported by the fact that conservative denominations did not decline, and, apparently, no one looked back at their growth rates in the 1950s and 1960s to see how much the rates had fallen.

The myth was also fostered by the increased visibility of conservative churches and conservative Christians through the use of religious television programming. It has been hard to ignore Jim Bakker, Jimmy Swaggart, Oral Roberts, Pat Robertson, and Jerry Falwell in recent years. Furthermore, some of the smaller conservative denominations *have* been growing very rapidly in the 1980s. By and large, however, the larger conservative denominations wish, like the mainline denominations, that they could return to the easy growth of the 1950s.

All major denominations were affected by the religious changes of the 1960s and 1970s—mainline and conservative alike. It is true, however, that the more liberal denominations were hit hardest by the changes. First, the growth rates of a number of these denominations were already quite low, so it did not take a major drop to move them from growth to decline. Second, members of liberal mainline denominations tended to have lower birth rates, on average, and a higher average age than members of more conservative denominations—making it essential that they hold onto the relatively sparse offspring of their members. Third, many mainline denominations had their greatest concentration of members in regions of the nation most profoundly affected by the cultural changes associated with the so-called counterculture. So even if we ignore the theological, stylistic, and other substantive differences between liberal and conservative denominations, mainline groups were at a clear disadvantage.

Then it happened. Membership decline became pervasive, but there was no mass exodus from the mainline denominations. In fact, the proportion of Americans who said that they belonged to mainline groups dropped very little during the 1970s and 1980s. This should have resulted in fairly rapid membership growth because the population of the United States was increasing at a steady pace. Growth did not occur, however. Larger and larger numbers of Americans said that they belonged to mainline denominations, but growth came only in the form of Mental Members rather than in the form of participating members who could be found on the church rolls.

Persons who identified with the Episcopal Church, for instance, made up approximately 2.7–2.9 percent of the United States population in the mid 1960s. By the mid 1980s this proportion had dropped to 2.4 percent. By maintaining this proportion of a growing United States population, the Episcopal Church should have grown almost 21 percent over this period. Instead, it declined by 26 percent.

During the 1950s and early 1960s, the majority of persons who said that they were Episcopalians were, in fact, members of Episcopal churches. Since that time the proportion of Episcopalians who identify with the church but who are not members (Mental Members) has expanded greatly—from roughly 4 percent in 1964 to 17 percent in 1973, to 48 percent in 1977, and to 71 percent in 1986.

Among Lutherans the situation was similar. In 1957 only 9 percent were Mental Members. This proportion soared to 35 percent by 1973 and to 49 percent by 1986. The same pattern can be found among many other denominations, although measuring the change is very difficult for most religious bodies due to lack of adequate numbers from national polls and problems with membership records.

More Americans apparently drifted away from mainline churches than consciously dropped out. Youth left home and promptly forgot about the church. Adults changed jobs and neglected to change churches when they moved to a new city. Nearly all of these people retained a church identity. Yet they never re-affiliated with new congregations and were eventually dropped from the rolls of their former churches.

For a denomination to grow, it must hold onto its members both in terms of identity and in membership. This has not happened, and there is evidence that this inability to keep members from drifting away has affected mainline denominations to a greater extent than conservative denominations.

The two predecessor denominations that became The United Methodist Church, for instance, received by letter of transfer nearly 400,000 persons in 1952. This number declined to 362,000 in 1965, to 274,000 in 1974, and to 234,000 in 1987—dropping nearly one half. In contrast, the Southern Baptist Convention received additions by letter or statement totaling 472,000 in 1953. Such additions rose to 527,000 in 1974 before dropping off slightly to 489,000 in 1987. The United Methodist Church is not holding onto its members very well, nor is it attracting as many members from other denominations as it once did. The Southern Baptist Convention has never been particularly attractive to the members of other denominations, but it does tend to hold onto its own.

How did the liberal mainline denominations respond to the problems they were facing? They made matters worse by embracing countercultural values and by ignoring the very activities that would have slowed the losses. The term *evangelism* fell into disuse in some denominations and took on new meaning in others. Budgets for new churches were slashed, resulting in huge drops in "church planting" (the Methodists, for instance, started 199 churches in 1955, but only 16 in 1971). Sunday school was weakened by the redefining of its goals and by the replacing of traditional age-graded classes with short-term courses.

It soon became clear that the losses were not an aberrant pattern that would quickly go away. But instead of repairing the damage to growth-producing denominational structures, apologists helped the losses to become sources of pride as they spoke of "getting rid of the deadwood" or "being true to ourselves and God." This allowed the problems to continue unabated for years. By the time church leaders at the national and judicatory levels came to their senses and began to reemphasize evangelism and church planting, too much damage had already been done for any kind of a "quick fix" to work.

Even today many high-ranking program personnel in mainline denominations seem to be more concerned about the impact of the membership losses on operating revenue and the subsequent loss of regional and national staff than about what the losses really mean—a decline in the ability of mainline denominations to reach the unchurched with the gospel and to hold onto their own members.

Why Did They Leave?

Dropouts leave the church for a variety of reasons, and they stay away for still others. Some of the reasons dropouts give may be true, whereas other reasons are only rationalizations. These stated reasons for leaving and the characteristics that dropouts and *Nones* share will be considered in later chapters. The concern here is why so many dropped out of the church or simply drifted away during the 1960s and 1970s.

The religious revival of the 1950s ended years before the period of intense social unrest and denominational decline began. Perhaps it was inevitable. Church participation and church membership reached all-time highs in the late 1950s and were maintained, at least in part, by a tenuous link between the popular culture and the church. America, the family, and the church were in lockstep—headed in the same direction. Eventually, this artificial unity began to erode, perhaps because the ideals of the era were so unrealistic. Prosperity did not come to all, family life was not like the movies, and the church could not deliver as much as it seemed to promise. Religious activity began to decline slowly—a drop that was accelerated by the emergence of the counterculture and its anti-institutional values.

The 1960s and early 1970s were periods of intense social unrest. Anyone who lived during this time cannot forget the protest marches, the race riots, the endless Vietnam footage on television, the hippies of Haight-Ashbury, the deaths at Kent State, the Chicago Seven, and the diffusion of drugs across middle-class white America. Anyone who was a college student at the time cannot forget the fear of being drafted, the shock of hearing professors tell us we were fighting for the wrong side, and the experience of living in a time of changing social and moral values. Everything was suspect and much was found wanting.

The comfortable suburban churches which had flourished in the 1950s seemed to have little to offer the youth of the 1960s. A counterculture emerged which rejected the overt materialism and complacency of the previous generation. Although the counterculture lacked the structure to maintain itself as a viable alternative to the dominant culture, it did leave its mark. Steven Tipton describes the aftermath of the sixties in this way: "The conflict between utilitarian culture and counterculture of the 1960s left *both* sides of the battlefield strewn with expired dreams and ideological wreckage."[20] The counterculture stripped the moral authority and respect from government, law, business, the family, and the church—especially in the eyes of young Americans.

A great number of young Americans believed that the church represented irrelevant tradition. For many youth, religion in mainline churches was hypocritical, bureaucratic, moralistic, overly rationalistic, and wholly unconcerned about the injustices that were so readily apparent in America. Countercultural youth who sought greater freedom of expression in their religion found warm welcome in religious cults and communes. These youth were the minority, however. The bulk of those who became disillusioned with the church simply left. Some gave a shrug of disinterest as they drifted away, while others shook the dust off their feet.

Countercultural values also spread in diluted form to older generations. Few older adults became true dropouts, but millions eventually drifted into Mental Member status after they began to see church involvement as optional or irrelevant. Some remained church members, while an increasing number of others became lost to their churches and eventually were purged from the rolls.

At the same time that these cultural changes impacted the nation at large, other events—the Second Vatican Council (1962–1965) and Humanae Vitae (the encyclical that reemphasized the church's ban on mechanical and chemical contraception in 1968)—impacted only Catholics. These historic events sent to American Catholics the contradictory messages of increasing openness and restricted freedom. Dissent became possible within the church, and, at the same time, a virulent reason for dissent emerged. As a result, those who opposed the church on its stances regarding women in ministry, birth control, divorce, religious intermarriage, and church authority felt free to do so publicly. Some Catholics even felt strongly enough to leave the church—an act which now seemed to hold less serious consequences.

In addition, changes in official Catholic positions regarding the sinful nature of certain acts, such as eating meat on Fridays, raised questions about the attribution of sinfulness to other activities. As D'Antonio, Davidson, Hoge, and Wallace note, "The structure of blind obedience to external authority was undermined."[21] Mass attendance and confession were among the activities that suffered as a result of these changes. Many Catholics assumed that missing weekly Mass was no longer condemned as a mortal sin, whereas other Catholics simply felt a new freedom to reject the teachings of the church in this area. With this pattern operative, and with the impact of countercultural values upon Catholics as well as Protestants, many Catholic youth and young adults began to move closer to their Protestant "cousins" in terms of worship attendance patterns. The net result was a drop in church attendance among Catholics which was much more serious than that among Protestants.[22]

Will They Return?

The United States may never return to the level of religious participation prevalent in the 1950s—when 98 percent of the population held a religious identity and 49 percent attended church on an average Sunday.[23] In fact, this era may have been an anomaly which could be sustained only when religion and the dominant culture were linked very closely (perhaps too closely).

The years of easy growth may be over, but some true dropouts and many Mental Members will undoubtedly return to the church. According to the 1988 Gallup Unchurched American poll, one quarter of churched respondents have had periods in their lives when they have not attended religious services for two or more years, and the majority of these persons experienced these periods when they were less than thirty years of age.[24] This means that many persons who are active church members now were dropouts or Mental Members as young adults. They returned to the church, and the same will be true for thousands of presently unchurched Americans.

The question remains as to which churches will be able to attract the dropouts. Rarely do dropouts return to the congregations they have left, and many do not even return to the same denomination. Will they be attracted to your mainline church, or will they be drawn to that huge independent church overlooking the interstate, or to the church of that television preacher, or even to that house church network which has been silently expanding throughout the city? This is one of the questions that pastors, church staff, and lay leaders must ask themselves. If the answer is no, they will not return to our church, then a follow-up question must be asked: Is it because of who they are, or is it because of who we are? The most honest answer to this question is a little of both.

The dropouts are hard to reach because of their values, attitudes, and life-styles; and their possible reentry into the church is restricted because the traditional ways of "doing church" are unattractive to those whom one independent church pastor calls "unchurched Harrys."[25] The perception that has been created is that no one is being successful at reaching unchurched baby boomers. But this perception is false. Baby boomers are being reached in large numbers by "market-driven" independent churches and non-traditional denominational churches. Although there are relatively few of these congregations in any one city, they are effective because they respond to the felt needs of the unchurched and they create new patterns of worship and church structure which attract rather than repel the unchurched.

Efforts by all churches to reach dropouts and other unchurched must begin now for two reasons. First, many of these persons are still young and remain open to changes in attitude and behavior. This openness will decline steadily as they age. Second, many of those who have dropped out in terms of participation still identify with the churches of their youth. This identification will not last forever, however, and churches must begin the process of reclaiming their own before these persons are lost for good.

Time is short. The baby boomers who contributed so greatly to the expansion of the dropout population are aging.

Many are no longer young adults. Also, there is evidence that mainline Mental Members are beginning to lose their nominal commitment to their former churches and are now shifting out of the mainline in various directions.[26]

Renewed efforts must be made to reach those who are outside the church—those who were once active church members and also those who have never been "churched." These persons will be difficult to convince, and the changes needed may be uncomfortable, but the effort must be made. There are simply too many dropouts in this society for the church to ignore.

We start by understanding those who have left. The next chapter takes a look at the largest of this group: persons who are halfway out and halfway in the church. I call them Mental Members.

II

Mental Members

The largest group of unchurched Americans are the Mental Members—persons who say that they are Episcopalian, Church of Christ, Catholic, or something else but who rarely, if ever, attend church. They are the Lutherans who attend only on Christmas or Easter. They are the Catholics to whom Catholicism is more of an ethnic identity than a religious preference. They are the Presbyterians who dropped out of the church when someone made them mad. They are the Disciples who say that they will attend church again when they find a Disciples of Christ church nearby (but who never bother to look for one). They are the agnostics and atheists who still find a religious identity somehow comforting or meaningful. They are "solitary Christians" who believe that church participation is irrelevant to their faith.

Mental Members can be defined in a variety of ways. The definition used here is persons who say that they are Protestant or Catholic but who attend religious services less than once a year. By this definition, 17.7 percent of Protestants and 13.2 percent of Catholics are Mental Members. This translates into approximately 25.6 million adult Americans (19 million Protestants and 6.5 million Catholics).[1] Of all the unchurched, Mental Members are the most similar to active church members in terms of their attitudes and social characteristics and also are the most likely to return to active church participation.

Who are the Mental Members?

Mental Members have many characteristics that are similar to active Protestants and Catholics. They are just as likely to be young, to live in large cities, and to have been reared in affluent, well-educated families as are active church-goers.[2] On the other hand, differences do exist—some which are striking and others which are more subtle. For instance, Mental Members are more often male than female. This is probably true because the very religious male has the cultural image of being weak and somewhat repressed and also because of traditional role functions prescribed for males and females. It is acceptable to be a Methodist, but, in many sectors of society, being a *very religious* Methodist is not encouraged. The western states also have a disproportionate share of Mental Members. Unlike the rest of the nation, the West never experienced a "great awakening" and therefore retains some of its unchurched frontier character. Lower levels of church involvement are considered to be normal in the West, just as active church membership is considered to be normal in the South.

White Protestants are much more likely to be Mental Members than are black Protestants. The black church is such an integral part of the black community that it rarely would be viewed as irrelevant or unnecessary. It also may be that a smaller proportion of blacks have gone far enough "up" the social scale in this society to be "up and outers"—in the sense of moving out of religion altogether when an even higher status church cannot be found. In any event, blacks are more likely to have a religious preference than are whites, and black Protestants who have a religious preference are more likely to attend church regularly than are white Protestants.

It is easy to construct an image of the Mental Member as

an educated, middle-class white male who identifies with the church for social reasons. The fact is, Mental Members tend to have somewhat lower education and less occupational prestige than the typical active Protestant or Catholic. The differences are not extreme, however, and it should be noted that Mental Members are not more likely to come from families with lower status. These differences between Mental Members and active Protestants or Catholics emerge later in life.

One of the key background characteristics shared by Mental Members is that many Protestant Mental Members are married to Catholics, and many Catholic Mental Members are married to Protestants. Religiously mixed marriages create barriers which keep people out of the church. Not only do such marriages have the potential for conflict over where the couple will attend and send their children, but mixed marriages also create the potential for lack of acceptance. Churches are often hard for anyone to penetrate, and they are especially hard for those who are "different" to penetrate.

Mental Members tend to come from less religious family settings. Few Mental Members said grace before meals while growing up, and most had parents who attended church infrequently. Fathers of Mental Members were less likely to attend church than mothers, but this was also true for active church participants. Neither the father's attendance nor the mother's attendance appears to be more salient to the eventual religious activity of their offspring. Rather, the religious example set by both parents is important.[3]

For Catholics, divorce has a major impact on religious status. Catholic Mental Members are more likely to have been divorced at some point in their lives than are active Catholics. Furthermore, a disproportionate number of Catholic Mental Members are reared in homes disrupted by divorce. The serious implications of divorce among Catholics evidently caused the parents of some future Mental Members to drop out of the church. As a result, their children lacked both the tradition of church participation and the example of their parents' regular church attendance. So one legacy of divorce among Catholics is offspring who only mentally affiliate with the church.

Mental Members tend to have attitudes that are more libertarian than liberal. They believe that people should be free of constraints. Mental Members are more likely to approve of premarital sex, extramarital sex, abortion, and the legalization of marijuana. On the other hand, Mental Members often have a less positive view of Jews, are no more politically liberal than active church-goers, and are much less likely to attend church with blacks.

The permissive attitudes of Mental Members carry over into their behavior. Mental Members are more likely to drink, to get drunk, to smoke, to go to bars frequently, and to have had sex with more than one person during the past year (for those who were sexually active). This life-style may be appealing to some, but it generally does not bring greater happiness. Mental Members tend to be less happy and are less satisfied with most aspects of their lives than are active Protestants and Catholics. Many are apparently "social isolates." They do not tend to join social groups or spend much time with their families, their neighbors, or even their friends. They go to bars more often and are more likely to have been beaten, shot at, and arrested.

The variety of factors associated with being a Mental Member suggests that more than one type exists. This appears to be the case since a statistical technique called *cluster analysis* has revealed three distinct, easy-to-understand groups: the Estranged, the Indifferent, and the Nominals.

The Estranged

"No, I don't think that membership means I'm a better Christian. I feel that we live perfectly good Christian lives as it is, and I think that we do good and I don't think we have to be a member of the Church."[4]

Americans have a rather individualistic approach to religion. Even the majority of active church members (67 percent) think that "a person can be a good Christian or Jew if he or she doesn't attend church or synagogue."[5] Such a view is even more widespread among the unchurched.

Because most people consider the church to be an optional part of being a Christian, large numbers of believers have left the church and see no compelling reason to return. They have become private Christians who worship God alone or who retain an image of themselves as religious, even though they do not express their religion in the form of church involvement. Most of these persons fit the profile of Estranged Mental Members.

The Estranged are persons who have had religious experiences, who feel a commitment to Christ, who believe in Jesus, who say that they pray to God, and who consider religion to be an important part of their lives. In short, they seem to be religious people. So why are they not in church? Like most churched persons, the Estranged believe that church participation is optional; but, unlike active church-goers, they have found a reason for exercising the option not to attend. They have some "beef" with the church and use it as a reason, an excuse, or a rationalization for not attending.

Many of the Estranged in America have a generally negative view of the church. For instance, 38 percent strongly agree that "most churches and synagogues today have lost the real spiritual part of religion," and 37 percent strongly agree that "most churches and synagogues today are too concerned with organizational [issues] as opposed to theological or spiritual issues." These percentages may not seem very significant, but it should be pointed out that only 30 percent of *Nones* strongly agree with the first statement, and only 25 percent of *Nones* strongly agree with the second statement.[6] In other words, even though the Estranged see themselves as somehow connected to the Assemblies of God, the United Church of Christ, the Reformed Church, or some other denomination or independent church, they are more likely to have negative views of the church than are persons who see themselves as having no religious identity.

The Estranged are more likely to identify with conservative or sectarian religious groups which give their members less latitude to "do their own thing." For instance, 70 percent of Mormon Mental Members and 54 percent of Baptist Mental Members were Estranged as compared to only 35 percent of Episcopalian Mental Members, 30 percent of Presbyterian Mental Members, and 23 percent of United Church of Christ Mental Members. Apparently, conservative Protestant Mental Members tend to remain outside the church because of specific objections, a general negative view of the church, and other problems rather than because they simply drifted away. They are religious people who are estranged from the church, rather than irreligious people who are indifferent toward the church.

Why are they estranged? The reasons are varied. Some are disillusioned like a woman from southern California who said, "I think the Churches have gotten like a lot of parts of society. They have to worry so much about paying the rent that they have forgotten the good news. They forget the evangelical message. They forget love."[7] Others feel that the church is too constraining and irrelevant: "I'd like to be able to be a part of helping, understanding, giving someone my time. If that is what my Church became, a part of me would be a part of that, because it is what God wants me to do. But, as long as it is going to be in rules or punishment—'I'll slap your hand if you do this,' or 'You are out of the Church if you do that'—no, I'll never be part of that!"[8]

Even though the Estranged hold religious values, they also value their freedom. Many Americans consider churches to be restrictive rather than empowering—telling them what they cannot do. Many Catholics tell horror stories about "frustrated old nuns" in parochial schools who slapped them for meaningless offenses or who saw sexual connotations in nearly everything. Similarly, those who were reared in conservative Protestant denominations may remember the long list of forbidden activities: dancing, drinking, smoking, "mixed bathing," going to movies, and so forth. For Mormons, the list was even longer.

The popular American image of an active church member is apparent in the characterization of such persons on television and in the movies. Active church members are somber souls who have been cowed by their restrictive churches. They are not allowed to have fun, so they repress their desires and pass judgment upon all who are not similarly repressed. This image scares many Americans away from the church. They say, "If I have to be like that, I just won't attend." After all, as we have seen, attendance is considered optional by most people.

Some of the Estranged are simply "burned out." Active church members are often overused by their congregations. Some essentially become codependent on the church and need the involvement (even though they may complain), whereas other people cannot say no and will accept job after job until they have had enough. Then they either switch churches or stop attending altogether. Retirees move to a new city and leave their committee chairs behind them. It is as though these Mental Members feel that they have "done their time" in the church and can now relax, go to the beach, sleep in on Sunday, go fishing, play golf, or work in their gardens.

Another large group of the Estranged feel that they have been wronged by the church or that the people there just don't care. Some say that no one came to see them when a family member died or when they were in the hospital. Others point to hypocrites in the church. As one man put it, "Church services in organized Christianity represent nothing more than a sacred canopy which covers the previous week's debauchery of its members."[9] Most of this group, however, simply were not welcomed by the church when a sense of welcome and acceptance was needed.

Finally, there are those whom the church has actually rejected or those who feel that they would be rejected if they tried to attend. "If you just got common clothes on, you see, a lot of them are going to look down on you and they kind of turn their nose up at you. . . ."[10] The poor, the homeless, those without "proper clothes," interracial couples, couples with religiously mixed marriages, cocktail waitresses, bar owners, people who work in liquor stores, homosexuals, alcoholics, drug addicts, and exotic dancers may feel rejected by the church—and many have been. These are people on the margins who have been rejected by most churches—especially by conservative churches. Your church may be open to marginal Americans, but does it consciously reach out to them? All persons, whether they are "like us" or not, should find welcome in our churches, as well as under-standing and help in time of need.

The Indifferent

The Indifferent keep their religion locked up so that it can't do them any harm (or good). Most believe in the resurrection of Jesus (83 percent) and pray to God (86 percent), but only a small percentage say that they have made a commitment to Jesus Christ; and none say that religion is very important in their lives.[11] They are not antagonistic toward the church; they just don't care.

One of the major sources of their indifference can be seen in the way that they were reared. The Indifferent were much less likely to have attended Sunday school or to have had any religious training as children than were active Protestants and Catholics. Furthermore, their parents did not attend church frequently, and religion was not important to most of them when they were growing up. They were reared by irreligious parents, they were inactive as children, and most of them were affiliated at one time or another with denominations in which the overall level of religious commitment was low. In short, the Indifferent were *trained* to be Mental Members, and they learned their lessons well. Ninety-six percent say that "a person can be a good Christian or Jew if he or she doesn't attend church or synagogue."[12]

The church faces a difficult problem when it must compete with recreation and relaxation for a group of people who are barely interested in religious matters. According to one Indifferent, "You've got so many choices here that my church is no longer the most important thing. . . . When it comes to priorities I come first. If I can't be happy myself, there is no possible way I can make my family happy. You find your own thing."[13] For the Indifferent, the choice is something like this: Should I attend a boring worship service and kill half the day, or should I have breakfast at the beach, or play a little golf? The beach or golf usually wins out, except on Christmas and Easter.

In addition to competition for time, there is the problem of pure apathy. One man said, "I feel religion is fine for some people, if you need it. Some people use it as a crutch. They need something to believe in. I believe in myself."[14] Another person said, "I just drifted away. I just stay away. I don't know what it would take to get me back."[15] This is typical. Because a firm commitment was not made early in life, there is nothing to hold the Indifferent in the church. The Indifferent view a worship service as a show that is meaningful to some people but not to them. They attend occasionally, but on most Sundays they either don't have the time to attend or would rather be doing something else.

The Indifferent are about halfway between active church members and *Nones*. They cling to a vague belief in God and are fairly orthodox in their perception of Jesus. At the same time, they are completely devoid of religious commitment and tend to hold rather liberal values concerning sexual freedom, abortion, and civil liberties. Only a small percentage of the Indifferent (14 percent) can imagine a situation in which they would become active members, yet 78 percent would like for their children to receive religious instruction.[16] They see value in what the church offers, and they want it for their kids. They probably do not want their kids to get too much of it, however—just enough to inoculate them with Christianity so they will catch its basic values but not the full disease.

Even though the Indifferent may not be able to imagine themselves returning to the church, they may, in fact, be easier to reach than many of the Estranged. The Indifferent believe in God and are not antagonistic toward the church. Reaching their children first through vacation Bible school, after-school tutoring or day care, church day camp, art classes, and Sunday school or church school is one approach that may help to reclaim some Indifferent parents and that also may prevent their children from growing up indifferent toward the church. Another is to show them that the church has something to offer other than boring worship and restrictive rules. This assumes, of course, that your church *does* have something more to offer. If it does not, efforts to reach the Indifferent will be futile.

The Nominals

It is hard to imagine why the Nominals bother to say that they have a religious preference. They not only avoid attending church but they also hold no traditional religious beliefs. They do not believe in the resurrection of Jesus, they never pray, they have not made a commitment to Jesus, they do not consider religion to be important, and most of them do not believe in life after death (only 16 percent do). In most areas the Nominals are less religious and orthodox in belief than persons who have no religious identity at all.[17]

The Nominals had irreligious parents, and they attended

church and Sunday school less than any other group while growing up, including the *Nones*. Like the Indifferent, the Nominals learned an uncommitted form of Christianity early in life; but, unlike the Indifferent, the only thing that the Nominals gained from their minimal association with the church was a denominational label.

It is likely that Nominals retain their religious identity primarily for status and cultural reasons. Many of the Nominals are older males with higher incomes and higher educations. Furthermore, Nominals tend to identify with high-status liberal denominations such as the Episcopal Church, the United Church of Christ, and the Presbyterian Church. So, rather than be honest and say that they have no religion, many status-conscious unbelievers mentally attach themselves to a high-status denomination that makes few demands.

Other Nominals have a rather free-floating set of religious beliefs. They hold extremely liberal values concerning sexual freedom and abortion, and they remain vehemently opposed to strict moral teachings in the church. Some have essentially constructed their own unorthodox form of belief by mixing Christianity with New Age thought and secular humanism. At one point in their lives they may have participated in a church that accepted them along with their unorthodox ideas. Now, however, they have drifted away, but they still retain an attachment to the church in which they once felt at home.

It will be difficult to reach the Nominals because of their skepticism toward religion and their lack of Christian belief. Still, it may not be impossible. Slightly over half want their children to receive religious instruction. They also appear to be very interested in social activities. They are concerned about meeting human needs in the community, about addressing public issues, and about cultural activities. Churches that offer programs in these areas and that are involved in community action are likely to be attractive to the

Nominals. At first, their participation is likely to be hesitant and their attitude suspicious. But, if trust can be developed, it may be possible to show Nominals the Good News—perhaps for the first time in their lives.

Churches can be seen as a series of concentric rings. The most committed, active members form the inner circle or nucleus. The next ring is composed of slightly less active members, some of whom are in the process of moving into the nucleus or out to even less committed rings. Even though churches use membership to distinguish members from non-members, some non-members may be closer to the "center" of the church than some members. At the outer edge of a congregation, the rings are less distinct and eventually fade away. Moving around this edge—not quite in the church and not quite out—are the Mental Members. Some don't want to be on the edge and are waiting for someone to show enough love to bring them back in. Others, however, think that the edge is the place to be. They either have drifted to this state of marginal commitment, or they have strategically placed themselves at the edge. In the gaps, outside the faded rings of any church, are the *Nones*. Chapters 4 through 8 consider these individuals. In the next chapter, however, the concern is how to reclaim Estranged and Indifferent Mental Members and how to reduce the parade of members from our churches who are joining their ranks.

Reclaiming Mental Members
(and How to Keep From Producing New Ones)

If you are a layperson, why do you attend church? Why do your friends go to church? Consider your motives carefully. To what extent do you and your friends attend because you feel that you should attend or need to attend rather than because you enjoy attending or get a great deal out of the experience?

A lawyer recently told me,

> I go to a large, active church where I have many good friends. The music is excellent there, and the pastor usually delivers an adequate sermon. Yet, to be perfectly honest, I have a more enjoyable time having brunch with friends, puttering in the garden, going bass fishing, skiing at the lake, and participating in many other leisure activities. I go to church because I think I should attend and because I need the experience of corporate worship. I attend my particular church because I have many friends there and because it provides the most enjoyable and meaningful Sunday school and worship services of the several Baptist churches my wife and I visited when we moved to town.

If this person did not feel that he ought to attend or that he needed corporate worship, would he still attend church? The answer is probably not. The experience is simply not enjoyable enough to compete with leisure activities, spending time with his children, keeping his house painted and his lawn mowed, and catching up on the sleep he missed during the previous work week.

Mental Members (and even many people who attend church regularly) view Sunday morning worship and Sunday school as activities that deduct from available family time, not as fulfilling family activities. Since the family is the greatest source of pleasure for most Americans (whether they are religious or not), family and leisure pursuits tend to win in the competition for weekend hours. The majority of Mental Members simply feel no sense of "ought" or "need" with respect to the church. So is it any wonder that they rarely, if ever, attend?

If church leaders understand the motivation and social characteristics of Mental Members, then it is possible to develop certain strategies for reclaiming the Estranged and the Indifferent which will help churches "slow the flow" of their members in this direction. That is the subject of this chapter. It should be noted at this point, however, that this prescription for action should be used as part of a well-thought-out plan to reach and reclaim specific types of unchurched Americans. All churches should have a ministry in place to reach into the unchurched community. The character of this ministry will differ according to the community setting, the types of members in the church, the openness to change that exists in the congregation, and many other factors. Church leaders should ask Whom do we want to reach and whom can we accept if we are able to reach them? Very large churches may be able to "do it all," but most congregations will need to be selective lest they have too many weak programs and no single ministry that is effective at reaching and reclaiming Mental Members, dropouts, or

Second Generation Nones. Whom does your church want to reach?

Reclaiming the Estranged

The Estranged have some "beef" with the church or stay out of the church because of a barrier that exists in their lives. Even though few of these fairly religious people feel it is necessary to worship in a church, many of them probably would like to resume attending—even though they might not admit it. However, first the barrier between them and the church must be removed.

The first place for a church to start the reclaiming process is with its own Mental Members, many of whom are Estranged. They are easy to find. One way to identify them is to conduct a church-wide visitation campaign. Active members can be recruited to make low-pressure "listening and caring" visits to all members on the church roll. Since those doing the visiting will not be asked to solicit funds or to evangelize, it usually is not very difficult to recruit members for this task. The results will be surprising. The church will discover many marginal members who are experiencing severe personal problems. These people are in need of ministry, but because they were never integrated into the life of the church and because they never asked for help, they were not supported by the "safety net" that the church provides for its own.

Other visitors will discover members who have dropped out some time ago for a specific reason and have been waiting to vent their anger, disappointment, or hurt to a representative of the church. It may be too late to reclaim some of these persons, however. John Savage says that churches need to deal with these problems within the first two months after someone drops out.[1] Still, if visitors can help to keep Estranged Mental Members from generalizing their "beefs" to all churches, these dropouts may eventually be open to the witness of another congregation.

On a recent building campaign for my church I visited two fairly active members of my own Sunday school class. I was very surprised to learn that the couple had not been attending for a few months and were thinking about looking for another church. They had no "beef" that they were willing to admit, but it was clear that they simply had never developed any close friends in the church. People were friendly, but the relationships were superficial. Well-integrated members take for granted that quiet persons who attend on a regular or semi-regular basis are satisfied and are committed to the church. This may not be true. I had been out of town too often that spring to notice that this couple was beginning to attend less regularly (I half expected to receive a visit from the pastor myself); but, in retrospect, I did notice that this couple did not appear to have any close friends in the class, and I suspected that they were not socially involved with any other members. Several members made efforts to reclaim this couple. It was too late, however. They were accepted, but they were never assimilated; and after they dropped out, all of the persuasive talk could not overcome the actions of the previous three years.

A program of visitation to each member will demonstrate that the church is concerned. It will deal with some minor "beefs" as visitors listen to stories of hurts and conflicts. It also will result in a list of persons with ministry needs and serious "beefs" that need the immediate attention of the pastor, church staff, and others.

The church can provide ministry to those who need it. Meals can be taken to the families of those who are ill. Concern can be expressed and support can be given to those who are experiencing trials. Counseling can be offered to couples with marital difficulties or to persons involved in substance abuse. Churches can and should meet these needs.

For those who are angry and hurt, additional visits from the pastor, a Sunday school teacher, and friends are in order.

If the hurt has not festered too long, such visits may be able to deal with the specific problem and reestablish trust.

Churches also may be able to reach Estranged Mental Members who are not on their membership rolls. This outreach can be done most effectively through the witness of individual members to their unchurched friends. More Americans attend church because they were invited by a friend or family member than for any other reason. Members can be trained how to share their faith in a low-pressure, non-threatening manner. The emphasis should be on providing a gentle witness to one's immediate circle of friends who are not Christians or who are no longer involved in a church. From there members can extend their witness to neighbors, co-workers, and casual acquaintances. This type of witnessing has been called *life-style evangelism, body evangelism,* or *network evangelism,* and it is the primary vehicle through which the church can reach beyond itself into the larger population of unchurched. It also is the least threatening form of evangelism for the average Christian.

Evangelism to most Christians is passing out tracts on a street corner or trying to witness to strangers by going door to door. It is a word that scares people, especially in mainline churches. Even in conservative, evangelical churches there is much more talk about evangelism than there is evangelistic activity. The average Christian, who has not been trained how to share his or her faith, rarely will be motivated to witness to strangers. On the other hand, nearly any committed Christian can be motivated to tell friends about his or her relationship with Christ. This is true evangelism; it is effective evangelism; and it should be supported and constantly encouraged.

A more difficult strategy, but one that every church should consider, is a program of evangelistic visitation. In almost any church there are a few members who are willing to be trained in a more aggressive form of evangelism. They have the desire to reach others for Christ, but they do not know how to express this desire. A pastor or minister of evangelism can train a cadre of members who are willing to knock on the doors of strangers and to risk rejection in order to reach those who plan never to return to the church. It should be stressed, however, that members must be well trained, and that this training must include training by example. Pairing "old hands" with trainees during visitation is essential.[2]

Before members are willing to witness to strangers, or even to tell friends about their church, the church must have something that is exciting enough to share with others. If it does not, a church can rely on the motivations of guilt, duty, and concern for the lost; however, these motivations are not sufficient to maintain the enthusiasm of very many church members.

One church in North Carolina had been on a statistical plateau for six years despite tremendous population growth, a nice building, and a very visible location. Why did it fail to grow? Sadly, the members were embarrassed by the sorry state of the church, and they were not about to invite their friends to attend. Long-time members remained because they were committed to the congregation and had many friends there. One man told me, "What could I say to my friends, 'Come to church with me this Sunday . . . I hate it there, but you might like it'?" Finally, after an interim minister had healed the wounds, a new pastor was able to lead the church to amazing growth almost from the moment of his arrival. The growth came easily because everyone in the church who had suffered through the years of conflict was now gushing to friends about "my church and our wonderful new minister."

Not only must church members be willing to tell Estranged Mental Members about Christ and to help them overcome their past hurts and false impressions, but the churches also must have something to offer Mental Members when they do come to worship. Many of the dropouts will show up for Easter services, and others may attend periodically at the urging of their friends. How will they view your church when they come? Will the experience reinforce a stereotype that kept them away in the first place, or will it show them that all churches are not alike and that maybe the people here are OK? Above all, a church should be friendly and accepting to these newcomers, no matter how they look.

It is also essential that worship services are not boring. There must be life, meaning, and love; there cannot be condemnation. Unfortunately, the worship services in many mainline and conservative churches are very tedious affairs and are seen as such by many, if not most, Americans. For instance, in a recent episode of "The Family Feud" contestants were asked to "name a place where you get bored." The number one survey response to this question was work, but the number two response was *church*. This is sad, but it should not be any great surprise given the nature of worship in many churches. Most services consist of boring announcements, unexciting prayers, long hymns sung too slowly, an offering, and a vague moral message that exhorts members to be followers of Christ without telling them *how*. To the hearer the message is translated, "be nice people."

Other churches add recitations of "hip liturgy" or homemade responsive readings such as the following, which was used at a worship service in Indianapolis: "God of the springtime, I come, but the soil is not ready for planting, I am afraid of the future. God of the summer, I come, but I resist the sun and the rain, I don't like being exposed. God of the harvest, I come, but do not pick the fruit, if there should be fruit, I grew that fruit, it's for me. . . ." This is not what Mental Members want to hear, nor is it what many active members want to hear. The active members will stay (most will, that is) because of their feeling of "ought" and "duty," or because they simply don't know any better. But Mental Members will shake their heads and say, "It was worse than I remembered; how can those people sit through that boring stuff *every week?*"

Worship services can be celebrations. They can be exciting, moving, humorous, inspiring, and filled with expressions of love without becoming carnivals and without sacrificing meaningful liturgy or spirituality. Good examples can be found in cities and towns everywhere—many of which are not denominational churches. Independent churches that consciously engineer their worship services to be exciting and entertaining and to meet the felt needs of unchurched young adults, baby boomers, and their children are springing up in most major cities. Reaching the unchurched is the sole aim of these churches, and because they cannot rely on transfers from other churches of the same denomination, doing so is the only way they can survive.

One place for any church to begin is for church leaders to ask the members what they like (or do not like) about their church and its worship. This information will help a planning committee to know what must be kept and what might be changed. A second step is to ask residents of the community who are not church members what they would like to see in a church and why they do not attend your church. Changes can then be based on the needs of members and residents rather than on someone's perception of what people want in a church.

Who Will We Accept?

Some people legitimately feel estranged from the church because they indeed have been rejected, or because they have reason to believe that they would be rejected if they attended. The largest group of this type is composed of couples with religiously mixed marriages. Catholics who marry Protestants and Protestants who marry Catholics are often estranged from either church. Rather than converting to the faith of the spouse or attending church separately, many simply stop attending altogether.

When a Catholic husband attends a Protestant church with his wife and does not let anyone in his wife's church know that he is still a Catholic, he opens himself up to being offended when a Sunday school teacher—or even the pastor—mentions the Roman Catholic Church in a slightly negative manner. This happened in a Sunday school class at my church. The offended husband said, "I go to this church to keep my family together on Sunday, but I do not think anyone should criticize another denomination." Despite the teacher's apology and care to mention the Catholic Church in more positive terms, the couple began attending less frequently and eventually left the church. A Protestant who regularly attends a Catholic church might risk being similarly offended.

Clothes can be another source of estrangement. A number of unchurched persons interviewed by Russell Hale mentioned the elitist nature of many churches.[3] People who cannot afford nice clothes and large numbers of others who simply dislike wearing "church clothes" (and for this reason don't own any) feel excluded from the church because of the unwritten dress code. When living in Massachusetts for three years, I adjusted rather quickly to the prevailing norm in my college-town church to dress as you pleased. On nice days, most people wore "church clothes," but when it snowed or was ten degrees below zero, most of us wore boots, jeans, and long johns. After this experience, an adjustment to a middle-class church in Atlanta, where suits and dresses were *de rigueur,* came as an unwelcome shock.

This issue of dress is one reason that some adults find a Saturday evening or early morning Sunday worship service attractive. At these services women generally feel free to wear slacks and men can wear polo shirts. So even if worship attendance at your church does not suggest that a second service is needed, providing such an alternative may be a way of increasing the participation of marginal church members and of attracting new people.

Some churches exclude members of other races; most churches exclude homosexuals and exotic dancers. Baptist churches exclude people who work in the liquor and tobacco industries (except in some states). Whom does your church exclude, either consciously—by not allowing them to join—or unconsciously—by not providing for their needs or by failing to reach out to them? Are you excluding persons whom you would like to reach? Does your church exclude the handicapped because of your facilities? Do your programs for the elderly exclude elderly residents who did not grow old in your church? Do you exclude nearly everyone because only long-term members are accepted? By condoning all of these exclusionary actions, our churches add to the pool of Estranged Mental Members.

In our efforts to reach out and reclaim the unchurched, each congregation should consider who it will accept and what changes must be made to make these people feel at home. Does your church want to reach couples with religiously (or racially) mixed marriages? Is your church willing to consciously relax its dress code so that people without fine clothes will feel comfortable attending. Does your church want to minister to homosexuals? Before serious attempts are made to reach the Estranged, these questions must be answered.

An Ounce of Prevention

The Estranged left the church for a specific reason and now feel that they can get along without the church. Churches essentially create the Estranged. Churches do not do it intentionally, but religion, like politics, has great potential for making people mad. It always will; but perhaps churches can do something to keep the stream of Estranged to a trickle.

Conservative and sectarian religious groups have the most

serious problem of creating Estranged Mental Members. People leave such churches because they seem to be too restrictive and judgmental. In the movie *Footloose*, John Lithgow's portrayal of a repressed, neurotic minister in a small town in which dancing had been outlawed is a classic cultural stereotype of the conservative preacher. Even though few towns might actually ban dancing, many young Americans believe that their pastors would love to see it happen everywhere.

Clearly, conservative churches cannot suddenly loosen their moral code and say, "If it feels good, do it." Yet the primary emphasis of the church should not be on condemning sinful acts and those who commit them. "Sinners in the Hands of an Angry God" would not impress the unchurched of today. The emphasis must be on the positive—on the need to develop a relationship with a caring God—rather than on adding to a list of "thou shalt nots." Furthermore, pastors should become aware of the moral battles being fought by youth and adults today. Many conservative pastors are preaching against activities that are not condemned in the Bible and that their members think are acceptable. Oddly enough, the crucial moral issues of the day are rarely mentioned: drug abuse, sexual immorality, abortion, and questionable business practices. Other important moral issues such as racism and sexism are mentioned in some churches but not at all in others. Simply condemning sinful actions and those who commit them will only drive away the "guilty" persons in the congregation. Pastors should recognize that some of their members are presently involved in illegal or immoral activities, should gently tell them why this is not in their best interest, and should show them how to deal with the problem by making a conscious decision to change—*with* the help of their fellow Christians and the power of the Holy Spirit.

Another way that churches create Estranged Mental Members is by working members too hard. All too often members who accept one task are asked to do another, and another, and another. Some people have a hard time saying no and do a good job at everything they take on. The tendency is to overuse such persons. Unfortunately, these "saints" will not complain about the load, but they will grow to resent it. When they leave, they leave suddenly—when they complete a big job or move to another city. Some may switch to another church with a vow never to accept another job, but many simply drop out for a few years in order to recover. Elderly Mental Members who feel burned out from overuse may "retire from the church" and return only on Christmas or Easter to any convenient church near their new retirement home. Churches must keep an eye on the number of jobs assigned to their members and must set limits. One church in Los Angeles does not allow its Sunday school teachers to take committee assignments. Other strategies can be used. This should be an important concern because churches cannot afford to lose their most active and productive members.

Most members do not drop out even when their church makes them mad. Why? Because they are committed to the institution and have many friends there. Members who are well assimilated and feel loved by most of their fellow members will rarely leave because the pastor or someone else offends them. As Daniel Olson notes in his study of social networks, commitment, and church growth, "Church friendships appear to bind churchgoers to their church even in the face of dissatisfaction with other areas of church life."[4] Church members may try to persuade the offending party to leave (especially if it is the pastor), but they themselves will stay because they see the congregation and building as "my church." They have what Lyle Schaller calls "redundant ties"—a set of reinforcing links which bind a member to a particular church.[5]

What should a church do when members leave in a huff? First, the church must know that they left. In a large church, this takes good records and people to watch for dropouts. Second, the potential dropouts must be visited, quickly. If too much time passes, it will be too late to reclaim them. The fact that they left and that no one either noticed or bothered to ask *why* is confirmation that the members just don't care. A quick visit says that the church does care, that it wants to deal with the hurt, and that it is willing to restore the dropout into its fellowship.

Reclaiming the Indifferent

Indifferent Mental Members do not drop out in a huff; they just drift away. In fact, most never really dropped out in the first place—they are Second Generation Mental Members who were reared on the periphery of the church and have remained there into adult life. They were married in the church (or will be), they attend occasionally, and they are happy with this marginal status. To the Indifferent, the church is a service station to be used occasionally—when needed—but to be ignored the rest of the time.

Because the Indifferent are convinced that the church has nothing to offer them and because they are not seeking answers to ultimate questions, they will be difficult to reach. They must be coaxed back to the church, and they must be shown that the church has more value than they ever imagined.

One proven strategy for reaching the Indifferent is focusing on children from the local community, many of whom will come from unchurched families. Sunday school, backyard Bible clubs, and vacation Bible schools are traditional vehicles for reaching the children first. Parents may see the excitement of their children and may wonder if this church is as irrelevant as they had thought. The activities for children should include some kind of special event that brings the parents to the church for a program. This overcomes one of the major barriers that keeps many people out of the church: fear of the unknown. Once inside, the church becomes familiar to the parents, and they find that returning to the setting is not so difficult. As James Kennedy notes, however, "This source [parents of children who attend Sunday school] will not prove very fruitful unless Sunday school teachers have had an active program of visiting in the homes and showing an interest in the children's progress in their Christian education."[6]

Bilingual Baptist Church in Pico Rivera, California, extends the concept of "reaching the children first" through their summer-long preparation for an elaborate musical production—complete with a large set, complex choreography, difficult acting parts, and musical solos. Kids are expected to participate five days a week from nine o'clock in the morning to noon—with only three absences allowed. Because the production is open to the community, a substantial number of the participants are from unchurched families. Several performances are held at the end of the summer, which draw even more unchurched residents. Over the past ten years the church has seen many dropouts and Mental Members slowly become part of the life of the church through this musical production.

When unchurched persons have been asked about church-related programs that might interest members of their immediate families, the number one response has been summer programs for children (22 percent of unchurched persons who had once been more active in the church than they are now gave this response). In contrast, only 9 percent expressed interest in a neighborhood Bible study, and only 6 percent expressed interest in church school. Churches cannot afford to neglect this avenue of entry into unchurched families.[7] Even if unchurched parents are not reached in all cases (and they will not be), their openness to church participation on the part of their children allows these children to be exposed to the church during a time in their lives when important values and ideals are being formed.

This may prevent many children from following their parents' lead and becoming indifferent toward the church.

Another way that Bilingual Baptist Church reaches into the unchurched community is by sponsoring a support group for parents of preschoolers. Child care is provided for these once-a-week sessions, which offer speakers on topics of interest such as the strong-willed child, toilet training, sibling rivalry, dealing with tantrums, and other issues that are of great concern to parents locked in combat with devious two- and three-year-olds. In addition, the group allows parents to share experiences and to receive support from others who are going through the same trials. The ministry shows that the church cares and that it is not concerned with irrelevant matters, and the parents' weekly contact with the church setting and its members makes the church more familiar and approachable.

Many other strategies can be used to reach Indifferent Mental Members. A church should examine its strengths and priorities in order to develop activities that would be of interest to its own marginal members and to others in the community. Groups might be organized to help the homeless, to combat drug abuse in the community, to provide literacy training, to raise funds for social action, and to do a host of other things. Some churches hold classes on ordinary topics in members' homes or shops: tuning up a car, growing vegetables, working with stained glass, smocking children's clothes, and so forth. Such activities may already exist in your church, but they may not be employed as vehicles for outreach.

The key is to get unchurched persons involved in non-threatening, non-judgmental relationships with Christians so that they can see the fruits of a strong commitment to Christ and of active church involvement. This may be enough to motivate Indifferent Mental Members to take a second look at the church; however, efforts to reclaim these individuals cannot stop there. Newly interested Mental Members must become involved in church-related groups so

61

that they can begin to develop reinforcing bonds to the church and to church members. The best way that this can be done is through involvement in a newly formed task-related group of some kind. In such a group the newcomer quickly becomes an insider rather than an outside spectator. Furthermore, by focusing on a task, the newcomer cannot sit back and observe. He or she must get involved in the task and thereby interact as a peer with other group members. In the process, the newcomers may acquire new skills or knowledge and may find, to their surprise, that the church is doing things that are important, that the members will accept outsiders, and that they have enjoyed participating. Their tentative courtship with the church may then result in something more permanent.

In this reclaiming process the church should remember that the Indifferent hold very liberal values in the area of personal morality. They will tune you out at the first mention of sin and will leave at the first hint of condemnation or judgment. They need to see what the Christian life has to offer before they learn what it costs. If we first show them the costs, they will not stick around because they will not believe that there are any meaningful benefits.

The true "apathetic and bored church member," to use the title of the book by John Savage,[8] cannot be reclaimed easily with a few visits, because these individuals do not drop out as much as they drift away. They have no "beef" with the church, and repeated visits to "find out what is wrong" only irritate them. For this reason, visitors in a church-wide visitation campaign should be taught to distinguish between the Estranged and the Indifferent. If visitors cannot do this, they may do more harm than good and may drive the Indifferent even farther away from the church.

Preventing the Production of Indifferent Members

Producing Indifferent members is a major problem for Protestant churches, especially for liberal mainline churches.

One reason is that some churches give the impression that the substance of belief is relatively unimportant. Pastors are often vague about teaching specific Christian beliefs because they have been taught not to be dogmatic about such things. People grow up in these congregations not knowing what to believe. So they develop an amorphous set of weakly held values drawn from the church, from popular culture, and often from Eastern mysticism. Commitment remains low because members are unsure about what they are committed to.

Whereas conservative churches tend to drive out some of their members because of their tendency toward dogmatism and moralism, less conservative churches are much more likely to suffer a *drifting away* of their members. This is especially true among the youth, who often "graduate from church" at the same time that they graduate from high school. They go away to college or move away from home and never find their way into a new church. In a recent survey of youth in five mainline denominations—the Christian Church (Disciples of Christ), the Evangelical Lutheran Church in America, the Presbyterian Church (U.S.A.), the United Church of Christ, and The United Methodist Church—it was discovered that 37 percent of youth age twelve to eighteen who are currently involved in the church do not expect to be active church members when they reach the age of twenty-one.[9] This shocking figure shows that our churches are becoming almost as successful at producing Indifferent Mental Members as they are at producing active church members.

This is a denominational problem as much as it is a local church problem, and it calls for action at both levels. Denominational leaders must move their agencies and boards back to the central purpose of the Christian church, back to meeting the needs of their constituents, and back to the "nuts and bolts" activities that keep a religious institution healthy.

The central focus of all denominations must return to unapologetically teaching and sharing the Christian faith. Members must come to know and understand the beliefs that set Christians apart from the followers of other faiths and from the secular culture. They still will be free to accept or reject these beliefs, of course, but at least they will know what it means to be a Presbyterian, a Disciple, or a Brethren. Furthermore, they must be taught why evangelism not only is important to denominational survival but also is central to their calling as Christian believers. Pastors, church leaders, and Sunday school teachers can do their part at the local church level. Members and the children of members must be shown that the church is more than a social club with religious symbols.

People attend church to have a sense of meaning and belonging. We have the belonging part largely under control, but meaning has slipped away. The church should help members encounter and come to know a real and personal God. There must be substance to their faith. Without substance there is nothing for youth to commit themselves *to*. Is it any wonder that so many youth drift away when their parents no longer force them to attend every Sunday?

With effort at all levels, denominations in this nation can recover what many have lost—a clear identity and purpose. Each group—whether liturgical or not, high church or low church, connectional or congregational—has something unique and positive to offer the unchurched and "barely churched" in America. It is time for the offer to be made.

IV

Young Dropouts

Nearly all Americans have a religious identity of some sort. When asked, "What is your religious preference?" by a polling organization or by someone from a church conducting a community religious census, most people respond, "I am Church of God," "I am a Nazarene," "I am a Lutheran," and so forth. Only approximately 8 percent will say that they have no religion at all.[1]

Of this 8 percent who are *Nones* (about 14½ million adult Americans), the majority were reared in some religious group.[2] That is, when these *Nones* are asked what their religion was when growing up, most say that they were "something" rather than "nothing." Not only are most *Nones* church dropouts, but most *Nones* are also young—73 percent are less than forty-two years of age.[3]

It is popularly assumed that youthful rebellion is a primary cause of dropouts from American religion, and that once these young people "sow their wild oats," settle down, and start a family they will return to the church. For this reason, all of the declining mainline denominations are waiting for some sign that their lost baby boomers will finally return to the fold.

There is some evidence that youth in America do lower their church participation for a few years before returning to active involvement. Studies have shown, for instance, that church members who report having left the church for two or more years usually did so in their late teens or early twenties.[4] However, there is also evidence that suggests that this pattern of leaving the church and returning later operates primarily for Mental Members rather than for true dropouts.[5]

Over the past several decades there has been an increasing tendency for young Americans to drop out of the church completely—to totally renounce any identification with the Christian church. Although this trend has abated somewhat in recent years, it has left a huge population of baby boomer dropouts, most of whom will be very resistant to efforts to bring them back into the church. As shown in chapter 1, the proportion of each age cohort that has no religious identity becomes "set" while they are young, and it does not change much as the cohort ages.

The large group of youthful dropouts poses a great challenge to the church. Can past patterns be overcome, or has the character of religion in America changed for the long term—inching closer to the secularism that is so prevalent in western Europe? The stakes are high. The United States once had only 2 percent who were *Nones*. As a result of cultural changes in this society and inappropriate actions of American churches, the percent of the nation's adults who have no religion has risen to 8 percent. Will the next upheaval raise this level even higher, or will American churches buck the trend and lower this percentage over the next several decades?

In order to design meaningful strategies to reach the large population of young dropouts, it is necessary that they be understood. Who are they, what are they like, and why did they reject the "faith of their fathers" (and mothers)? To help answer these questions, this chapter divides young dropouts into four groups, each of which is described in detail. The groups were identified through a complex statistical procedure called cluster analysis according to responses given to eleven questions on a nation-wide survey of Americans conducted by the National Opinion Research Center at the University of Chicago.[6]

Successful Swinging Singles

Successful Swinging Singles are cosmopolitan, single, and doing well financially. As is true with all four of the groups described in this chapter, they are also quite young (85 percent are adults age 38 or younger).

One of the key characteristics of this group is financial success. Figure 1 shows that the majority of Successful Swinging Singles (84 percent) say that their financial situation has been getting better over the past several years. This is in contrast to only 38 percent of persons who have remained in the church. Perhaps as a result of this upwardly mobile status, the majority of these dropouts are either "very happy" or "pretty happy." They are not as happy, on average, as persons who retain a religious identity, but, for dropouts, they are doing well.

Financial success and happiness probably have nothing to do with causing Successful Swinging Singles to leave the church. These characteristics do suggest, however, that most members of this group feel that they have little lacking in their lives and believe that they are on their way to even better things. Thus, they feel no need for the church and its ministries—even if they are inclined to consider investigating the church (which most are not).

The "swinging singles" aspect of this group can be seen in the fact that nearly all are single and most go to bars or taverns regularly. This is an active group with cosmopolitan life-styles. They are young and urban, they hold liberal values in regard to sexual activity, they are unfettered by marriage ties, they generally socialize with friends rather than family, and they have the money to finance their good times.

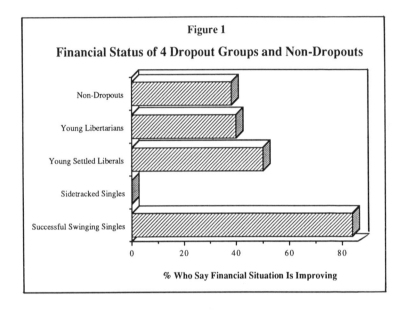

Figure 1

Financial Status of 4 Dropout Groups and Non-Dropouts

% Who Say Financial Situation Is Improving

Some of this group may fit Russell Hale's description of the "happy hedonist" who succumbs to the lure of leisure and the pursuit of parties. As one young man from southern California said in haste, "Just finished surfing this morning in the Pacific. Got to get to the mountains now to ski. . . . The churches can't compete with this!"[7] Successful Swinging Singles essentially combine unbelief with an active life-style which has no room for the church. All are not atheists, of course. About 49 percent believe in life after death. Yet it is likely that this belief, like the ill-defined belief in God so prevalent among the unchurched, is vaguely felt and lightly held. An engineer expressed this form of "half-belief" well when he said, "I have never thought that religion could solve my problems. I don't think I'm an atheist, agnostic perhaps, I just find it hard to talk about God."[8]

Perhaps the major reason for the rejection of the church by Successful Swinging Singles is found in their liberal attitudes about most social issues. Members of this group are highly educated, on average, and have adopted values that are in clear contrast to those of most Americans who attend church regularly. For instance, almost three quarters of these dropouts indicate support for the legalization of marijuana—as compared to only 21 percent of persons who retain a religious identity. Eighty-two percent support the right of a married woman to have an abortion if she does not want any more children. In comparison, 43 percent of church-goers express similar support. Successful Swinging Singles also are more likely to be political liberals than are most Americans, but the liberalism of this group is expressed most profoundly as liberalism in personal morality and social values. Successful Swinging Singles approve of premarital sex, and over half (59 percent) believe that homosexuality is not wrong. Their liberalism also extends to religious matters. As noted above, slightly over half do not believe in life after death. In addition, a majority approve of the Supreme Court's decision on school prayer and say that persons who are against churches and religion should be allowed to teach in colleges or universities—presumably influencing the next generation of young adults with their irreligious beliefs.

It is not surprising that this group left the church, given their attitudes and life-styles. They are now far from the church, separated by their values and activities. So why do they not seek out churches that share their liberal values? It may be that such churches are not reaching out to them. But it also is likely that Successful Swinging Singles lack a perceived need for the church and its ministries. In fact, the only characteristics of Successful Swinging Singles that suggest an opening for the church are that they are single and that a large proportion are not particularly satisfied with their family life (37 percent of this group express dissatisfaction in comparison to only 11 percent of persons who remain in the church). So even though many of these dropouts are quite satisfied with their financial situation, some have seen that material success and social activity do not ensure happiness in all areas of life. For those who want stability and the support of a "family," the church may be able to help meet this need.

Sidetracked Singles

Sidetracked Singles are similar in some ways to Successful Swinging Singles, but they differ dramatically in others—particularly in their financial condition and their general outlook on life. Similar to the first group of dropouts, they are young and unmarried; however, unlike Successful Swinging Singles, who tend to say that their financial situation is getting better (84 percent), none of the Sidetracked Singles report that their financial situation is improving. In fact, over half are not at all satisfied with their financial situation, and almost half say that their income is below average. These figures are in stark contrast to the responses of church members and even other dropouts. As I have noted elsewhere, "Even though the members of this group are young, apparently their lives have already been 'derailed.' They have been shunted to a sidetrack, watching the good life pass them by."[9]

Not only are Sidetracked Singles regressing financially, but they are also rather miserable. In fact, a rather grim orientation towards life sets this group apart from all other dropouts. From the data shown in Figure 2, it is clear that many Sidetracked Singles are very sad people and may need help. Sixty-three percent get no satisfaction to only a fair amount of satisfaction from their family life, and only 1 percent say that they are very happy (as compared to 36 percent of persons who retain a church identity). Their dissatisfaction and pessimism extend to virtually all areas of life. Most Sidetracked Singles are dissatisfied with their health, and 71 percent feel that the lot of the average person is getting worse.

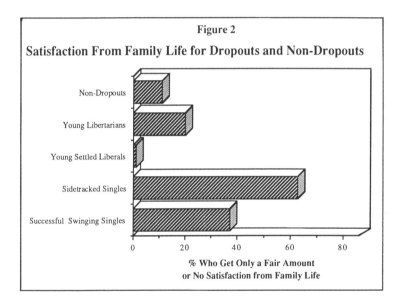

Figure 2

Satisfaction From Family Life for Dropouts and Non-Dropouts

It is somewhat difficult to estimate how much of the pessimistic view of life found among Sidetracked Singles is due to real difficulties and how much is due to perception.

There are people who look for the negative in every positive situation, of course, such as a friend of mine who complained about being sent by his business on a trip to Hawaii. Still, it is clear that unemployment is real (20 percent of Sidetracked Singles are unemployed in comparison to only 3 percent of the churched), as is being punched or beaten (73 percent of Sidetracked Singles have been abused in this way in comparison to 32 percent of the churched). Yet some people cope better with such problems than do others. Sidetracked Singles do not cope well at all. Instead, they generalize their problems to all areas of life and have difficulty finding solace for their troubles. They are unmarried, they lack close family ties, and they have rejected the church and the support that it might provide. They are on their own with their problems—and they are being overwhelmed by them.

Like Successful Swinging Singles, the source of conflict with the church for Sidetracked Singles can be seen in both values and behavior. Sidetracked Singles are highly educated and are very liberal in their views on social issues such as homosexuality, premarital sex, abortion, and the legalization of marijuana. In addition, 67 percent go to bars or taverns at least monthly in comparison to only 26 percent of churched persons.

It is also likely that the overall negative attitude of this group has been generalized to the church and to other institutions that represent the "system" that has treated them so badly. The world has done them wrong and has nothing good to offer. According to the Sidetracked Singles, the church—like many other things in the world—offers much but really doesn't care about people. As one recently divorced man expressed it, "Five years ago when I moved up here my idea was just to get away from a pretty sour society. I didn't see anything worth taking. . . . Now it's anything goes, just so you don't hurt anybody. It doesn't make any difference. God probably doesn't exist anyhow." In this brief testimony one can see the halfhearted agnosticism of most

Nones in America, coupled with a sense of pessimism. Whereas the Successful Swinging Single has no time for the church and no need for God, the Sidetracked Single has the need and, probably, the time but has rejected the church as a possible source of help—along with everything else. Sidetracked Singles believe that God, the church, women (70 percent of Sidetracked Singles are male), and their jobs (if they still have jobs) are to blame for their sorry state in life. These things are not to be trusted.

We can speculate that Sidetracked Singles would be very unlikely to return to the church because the barrier that keeps them away is composed of several reinforcing layers. This group holds values and exhibits behaviors that are much different than the average active church member, and they are further separated by their sense of pessimism. They are well educated, but the education has not paid off financially. They are single, but they are very unhappy with their family situation. They are young, but they are dissatisfied with their health. They want help and they need hope, but they remain apart from the two most readily available sources of help and hope: the family and the church.

Young Settled Liberals

Not all dropouts are young and single and are dissatisfied with their families. Young Settled Liberals, for instance, are married and have a greater sense of happiness and more satisfaction with their family life, on average, than do active church-goers. In addition, a large proportion of this group say that their financial situation is improving (second only to Successful Swinging Singles), and 64 percent find life to be exciting. In short, Young Settled Liberals have an extremely positive outlook on life which springs, at least in part, from a fulfilling marriage and satisfying family relationships.

It is normal to picture happy young families taking their kids to Sunday school, yet a number of other factors preclude such activity on the part of Young Settled Liberals. As their name suggests, they are very liberal in their views on most social issues. They support the right of women to have abortions for almost any reason and they tend not to condemn homosexuality. Just over half of them believe that marijuana should be legalized. In these and in many other attitudes, this group differs greatly from the constituency of most churches.

Young Settled Liberals are not "believers," but there is little evidence that they are personally "anti-religion." They may, for instance, allow their children to attend church. Some churches try to enroll the children of unchurched families when the parents are not interested. One dropout couple said that a Baptist church makes a big fuss about picking up their kids for church. Their response has been, "If they want to go, we let them."[10] This same couple, however, said that they can do without the church themselves, and that they have done so very well up to this point. Neighbors may ask such people to attend a special service now and then and may even witness to them about their faith. Young Settled Liberals are not hostile to such actions, and, in fact, are likely to attend once in a while out of curiosity. But their reaction to the experience is not what is anticipated. In the words of one dropout, "I found it all rather amusing."[11]

Young Settled Liberals make up the largest group of dropouts (29 percent) and are similar in many respects to Indifferent Mental Members (who were discussed in chapters 2 and 3). The majority of this group retain a vague, vestigial belief in God, but they see no need for worship or for a commitment to a religious institution. Like the Indifferent, they have drifted away from the church because of lack of interest, lack of common ground in the area of values, and the pull of other activities. However, unlike the Indifferent, they have severed their identification with the church of their youth. In this sense, Young Settled Liberals may be more honest than the Indifferent and certainly are more honest than the Nominals. Yet this honesty has separated them from the church to an even greater degree than these Mental Members by cutting off another source of commonality.

People who are active church members sometimes find it hard to believe that dropouts can be truly happy without the church. And, in fact, most dropouts are not particularly happy. Even though some dropouts are active and affluent, they have a nagging sense—when they slow down—that something is missing. For the Young Settled Liberals, however, family life has filled this gap with a sense of well-being and fulfillment. They have active lives, they are doing well financially, they are young and healthy, and they have the support provided by a stable marriage.

For most active, healthy, young people in this society, mortality is not yet an issue. They live "in the now" and do not concern themselves with the thought of death. They may have considered ultimate questions when they were very young, such as the source of life, the meaning of "forever," the nature of God, and the possibility of life after death. Now, however, these questions seem less compelling. The questions either have been answered well enough for the time being or have been "put on hold" until finally these individuals realize that they have fewer years to live than they have already "used up."

In a very real sense, Young Settled Liberals do not believe that they need religion or the church. They have reached the point where, as one young dropout said, "I just don't think religious thoughts, don't know when I last did."[12] Life is just too full and satisfying; and, like so many people, Young Settled Liberals tend to be nonreflective. Questions of ultimate meaning do not arise with much regularity. Furthermore, their active life-styles imply that they also do not need the church for fellowship. So they remain very resistant strangers to the church.

Young Libertarians

The fourth group of young dropouts is the smallest and the most unexpected (only 9 percent of all dropouts). Although Young Libertarians have many characteristics that are similar to other young dropouts, they are very unusual in two respects. First, they are very opposed to being constrained, and second, they retain a high level of religious belief while they totally reject a church identity.

I initially used the term *liberal* in the name given this group. Indeed, they are politically and socially liberal in many areas. Half support the legalization of marijuana in comparison to only 21 percent of church-goers. Well over half do not condemn homosexuality, and most (the largest proportion of any dropout group) think that the United States spends too much money on the military. Their liberalism is not consistent, however. Half oppose gun control (in comparison to approximately 28 percent of other dropouts and active church-goers). What's more, support for abortion is lower among the Young Libertarians than any other dropout group.

Young Libertarians dislike being told what to do and reject "labels" of any sort. This orientation toward freedom of action and thought is seen most clearly in response to a question concerning the ideal number of children for a family. Obviously, the liberal, socially conscious response would be to say "one or two"; but Young Libertarians do not give such a response. As shown in Figure 3, almost 90 percent say that the ideal number of children is either "five or more" or "as many as you want." Such a response starkly contrasts that of all other groups, including active church-goers. Unsurprisingly, many are former Catholics.

In the words of one Young Libertarian, "The church isn't

going to tell me how to vote, how many children I should have. That doesn't cut any ice with me, even if they quote the Pope in Rome. No institution is going to control me, even the church."[13]

This independent attitude carries over into all areas of the Young Libertarian's life, including politics and religion. I initially expected most dropouts to be Democrats, and, in fact, more dropouts are Democrats than are Republicans. The largest group, however, is made up of independents. Over half of the Young Libertarians (54 percent) say that they are independents or independents who are close to being Democrats in comparison to only 24 percent of church-goers.

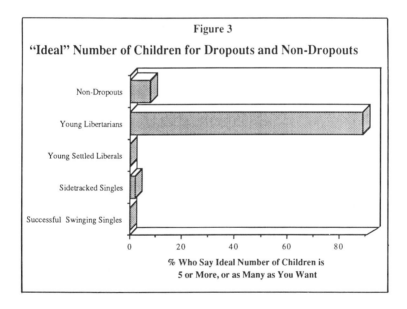

Figure 3

"Ideal" Number of Children for Dropouts and Non-Dropouts

% Who Say Ideal Number of Children is
5 or More, or as Many as You Want

When asked about their religious preference, all of the Young Libertarians said that they had a church identity when growing up but now have "none." For the other dropout groups, this rejection of a church identity in later life was

77

related, at least in part, to a rejection of orthodox religious belief. Yet when responses to a question about "life after death" are considered, it is evident that *a smaller percentage of Young Libertarians reject the idea of an afterlife than do people who retain a church identity.* Therefore, for this group, dropping out may be more of a rejection of a *religious label* than a rejection of *religious belief.* As one dropout said, "I think churches are pretty much social structures. I think many of them end up being social institutions instead of religious institutions."[14] For this person and many others, religion can be better expressed outside the church. Such persons see all of the institutions of society as constraining "boxes" to be avoided. In the words of one man from Oregon, "I remain flexible, mobile, fluid by staying outside. I make my own decisions. Boxes constrain me—even, maybe especially, the churches."[15]

Young Libertarians want to be their own persons, to live by their own rules, and to have a good time. A religious faith, however broadly defined, might be seen as a good thing by this group, but belonging to a church or even identifying with a religious denomination would be seen as unnecessary and pointless. Thus, Young Libertarians remain "outsiders"—a term coined for those who still believe but who no longer identify.[16]

There are other characteristics of Young Libertarians that may help us to understand this group. They are by far the most urban group of dropouts. Over half of them go to bars or taverns at least monthly. The majority of them are satisfied with their family life. Almost half of them were reared as Catholics. The percentage of Catholics is so high, in fact, as to suggest that some Young Libertarians may be considered "very estranged" former Catholics. They have totally rejected the authority structure of the Catholic Church, although they do retain some of its beliefs. As former Catholics, they cannot bring themselves to join another faith that might be somewhat closer to their own values.

Instead, they reject all such labels and say that they have "no religion." In the words of one former Catholic, "I'm a Christian—period. That has sustained me. All the other goodies I don't believe in at all." Like many others, this woman cannot join another church because "the indoctrination worked. . . ."[17]

The four dropout groups described in this chapter have some similarities and many important differences. In order to keep them distinct in your mind, you may wish to consult the chart on pages 124 and 125 which identifies the key characteristics of each group, as well as the other groups described in this book.

Other *Nones*

Not all dropouts are young. As will be explained in chapter 7, there is a group of older dropouts which differs greatly from all of the young dropout groups discussed in this chapter. Not only are they older, but they are also very traditionalistic in most areas of life. But, like the young dropouts, they also have rejected a church identity.

Chapter 7 also will consider persons who were raised with no church identity and who still have no church preference. Although these Second Generation Nones are not technically dropouts, they are an important part of the hard-core unchurched and should be understood.

In the next two chapters I turn from description to prescription. Can young dropouts be reclaimed by the church, and how can churches prevent potential young dropouts from leaving?

V

Reclaiming Young Dropouts

How many people have you known who have made a dramatic change in their lives—for the better? Do you know an alcoholic who became sober, or a drug abuser who became clean? Do you know a violent person who lost his desire to beat up others, or someone in the midst of a debilitating depression who regained her positive outlook on life?

Most of us could say that we know one or two persons who have undergone such a transformation, but we have met many more who have been unwilling or unable to alter their behavior or mental condition. Dramatic life changes are so rare, in fact, that when one does occur, it is cause for skepticism. I must admit that I was very skeptical of Charles Colson's conversion to Christianity. It seemed too convenient. Along with millions of others, I wanted proof of the change—the kind of proof that only time could bring. Yet the change did occur in Charles Colson's life. That it has lasted is cause for wonder—and for joy.

A similar reaction greeted the barrio students of Jamie Escalante in East Los Angeles. When eighteen low-income Hispanic students, some with gang backgrounds, passed the Education Testing Service advanced placement test in calculus, they were accused of cheating—even by those who had watched them give up their summer vacations, attend special classes on Saturdays, and study endless hours. In order to prove their accusers wrong, the students had to take the test again. This time the skepticism was replaced with wonder. How was it possible for a teacher to motivate basically uninterested students and to awaken a desire to learn so consuming that aimless barrio teenagers were transformed into fledgling mathematicians and were placed on the path to becoming physicians, lawyers, engineers, airline pilots, teachers, and other professionals? The wonder was so great that a movie was made about it—*Stand and Deliver*. See it if you doubt that people can change.

Just as educators assumed that barrio kids could not learn calculus, Christians also tend to "write off" hard-core dropouts, thinking that they will never change. Yet people *do* change, and, in some cases, the change is dramatic. Clearly, a dramatic change will be required for someone who has completely rejected the church to come to know Christ and to reestablish his relationship with the church. But if Jamie Escalante can turn barrio gang members into mathematicians, should it be so hard to turn Successful Swinging Singles into active Christians? Well, yes, it will be hard; but, unlike Escalante, we do not have to rely completely on our own skills and our own persuasiveness to convince others of the need to change. We have the Holy Spirit, who is also interested and involved in seeing the change and experiencing the wonder.

The Stakes are High

Even though there is the temptation to focus on "reaching the responsive" to the exclusion of dropouts and other hard-to-reach populations, such an action would be a dangerous mistake for churches to make. Over the past thirty years the United States has seen the proportion of persons who have no religious identity *(Nones)* expand from 2 percent to 8 percent of the population. In the latest Gallup poll data, the proportion of *Nones* among the youngest age cohort now stands at 14 percent.[1]

The trend for each new generation to be more secular than the one that came before has slowed, but it has not ended. The cultural upheavals of the 1960s and early 1970s made disaffiliation socially acceptable and thus increased the proportion of the population who claim no religious preference. This large group of new dropouts and the even larger group of Mental Members among older baby boomers is rearing a new generation that is even more secular than themselves. This new generation has not rejected the church because of countercultural involvement; rather, they are *learning* to be irreligious from their parents.

If those who are in their late teens and early twenties continue to have 14 percent *Nones* among their ranks, will this level become the next plateau of religious non-affiliation as the United States becomes more and more like England and the rest of western Europe?[2] Will the children of those who are now in their teens move American society to even higher levels of non-affiliation—perhaps to 20 percent or even 25 percent? The possibility is very real unless American churches are able to moderate the irreligiosity of young dropouts so that only a small proportion of this group will pass secularistic values to the next generation of young adults.

It is therefore *critical* that we understand young dropouts and how they may be reached. Evidence suggests that if young dropouts are ever to return to the church, they are most likely to do so when they are in their twenties and early thirties.[3] And while it is unlikely that a new religious revival will break out among this population, dramatic change in the lives of *individuals* is very possible. Each new convert or returnee will help to shrink the pool of dropouts, and the values that these individuals pass on to the next generation will be Christian values.

Capitalizing on Their Characteristics

At first glance, the characteristics of young dropouts appear to suggest few possibilities for reaching the four groups described in the previous chapter. Is there anything about Successful Swinging Singles, Sidetracked Singles, Young Settled Liberals, or Young Libertarians that will help to reach them rather than hinder evangelistic efforts among these populations? The answer is yes, but making the link requires some creativity.

One helpful characteristic is the prevalence of "transitions." Young adults are more geographically mobile; are beginning new careers; and are more likely to experience marriage, divorce or separation from their "partners," and the birth of a first child. All of these events are life-changing and can provoke subsequent changes in life-style and even in religious orientation.

Research data show that moving to a new residence in a different state is related to conversion *and* to disaffiliation.[4] In other words, *Nones* who move are more likely to convert than are *Nones* who do not move. It is also true that persons who were reared in the church and who move to a new city or state often use this event as an opportunity to drop out.

Churches must do a better job in keeping up with members who move and must become more aware of new residents in their communities. When a member moves, too often no effort is made to link him or her with a church of the same denomination in a new city. We leave it up to the individual to find a church. Many persons put this off for so long that they become accustomed to having their Sundays free. Eventually they are stricken from the rolls of their former congregations and never find their way into new churches. Also, relatively few churches make use of the various available lists of new residents. This is unfortunate because if dropouts can be contacted within a few months after moving to a new city, their need for relationships may overcome their suspicion of the church. They can be drawn into the fellowship of an accepting congregation and can begin to see that it really does have something to offer.

Marriage creates another opportunity for the church to impact those who were formerly outside its reach. Young dropouts are predominantly male, and most choose wives who do not share their radical rejection of religion.[5] Some will begin to attend church occasionally in order to promote harmony in the family, even though their heart usually is not in it. They may remain *Nones* in self-perception, but their very presence in the church gives Christians a unique opportunity to dialogue with them and to show them a more complete picture of Christ and the church.

In *Converts Dropouts Returnees,* Dean Hoge calls those who have returned to the church because of the influence of their spouse or out of concern for their marriage "Marriage Life Returnees."[6] Some of these returnees are religious seekers who, although interested in spiritual matters, never would have returned to the church on their own initiative. Other returnees have little initial interest in religion but are impressed by the faith of their spouse and eventually find their own faith rekindled. For still others, however, the return to the church is in body only. They remain dropouts by my definition, yet, unlike most other dropouts, they are in a position to hear the gospel and to see it expressed in the lives of Christians. Churches should be sensitive to the presence of irreligious spouses of members. They are in your church, observing with a critical eye and a skeptical attitude.

Children create additional opportunities for outreach efforts among young dropouts who are married or who were married at one time. Data from the Gallup Organization show that most unchurched persons want their children to be exposed to the church—presumably because they want their children to learn moral values and to make their own decisions regarding the church.[7] Few dropout parents teach atheism to their children. These parents are not hostile to the church. In fact, most think that the church is fine—for children.

Backyard Bible clubs, vacation Bible school, summer musical pageants, church camps, church retreats, bus ministries, and the like all can be effective means of reaching the children of dropout parents. The problem is how to reach the parents once the church has attracted the kids. Involving the children helps to familiarize dropout parents with the church; however, dropouts—unlike Mental Members—are unlikely to be drawn back simply because the place is familiar, the people are nice, and their children like the programs. Sensitive visitation to dropout parents is required by those who have the skills to engage them in nonjudgmental dialogue about Christianity and the church.

Dropouts are likely to be fairly ignorant about Christianity.[8] They have to be shown that Christianity is not a list of rules, and that it can be empowering, exciting, and full of meaning. They must be convinced, even though they will be a hard sell. Nevertheless, at least their children provide an opening into their lives which otherwise would have remained closed to any stranger who knocked on their door in order to "witness."

Single (never married) dropouts do not generally have children, but they do have other characteristics that may provide entry into their lives. One of the major characteristics of this group is an active life-style. Single dropouts are seeking a good time. A friend once suggested that a Christian singles bar might be a way to reach unchurched singles. As he described it, "They could sit around, drink beer, meet new people, and talk to Christians about Jesus." This friend, who eventually became a Presbyterian minister, never opened his Christian singles bar, but the purpose behind his somewhat harebrained scheme had merit—to somehow link Christian singles and non-Christian singles in a fun setting.

Some churches have had success using singles ministries

as vehicles to reach the unchurched. Such programs must have very active schedules of parties, outings, concerts, and the like if they are to have any hope of success. They also may include Bible studies, discussion groups, seminars, and issue forums. Dropouts may be drawn into these functions by Christian friends or by word of mouth (especially if it gets around that the singles group is a good place to meet girls or guys). Once a part of the group, dropouts are confronted with the reality of Christ as expressed in the lives of active Christian singles. Such proof can make their intellectual problems with Christianity seem irrelevant.

Other churches may use their involvement in social causes as a way of attracting dropouts. Whether the cause is helping the homeless, counseling drug abusers, protesting the involvement of the United States in Central America, teaching people to read, or some other issue, churches are likely to find socially conscious non-members or dropouts who are willing to join in their efforts. Frequently, the best way for this to happen is for the church to become involved in joint activities with existing groups in the community who share a common goal with the church.

Another non-traditional method of establishing contact with young dropouts is through the use of informational seminars on non-religious subjects or debates on controversial issues. First Baptist Church in Nashville, Tennessee, has sponsored a seminar on parenting for several years. The seminar is held on neutral turf (the convention center) and features well-known authors who address issues of concern to Christians and non-Christians. This seminar and another held recently on coping with divorce are open to the general public and are essentially a gift from the church to the city of Nashville. Events of this type can provide a first link to young dropouts. They show such persons that the church is not irrelevant, and they create a setting for dialogue between Christians and non-Christians. Misinformation about the church can be dispelled, paving the way for additional communication and influence. Other topics might include money management (a concern for Successful Swinging Singles), weight loss, investments, career planning, marriage enrichment, and so forth.

At the University of Massachusetts, Campus Crusade for Christ sponsored a debate between a representative of the Creation Research Society and a faculty member from the biology department. A huge crowd was attracted to the lively debate. Many, no doubt, expected to see the creationist "picked apart" by the evolutionist. The debate was heated, but it was thoroughly enjoyed by all of the students, who added cheers and boos as they saw fit. It also presented the opportunity for a brief presentation of a gospel message. Consequently, a large number of students requested additional information from the Campus Crusade staff. Debates on a wide variety of other topics, both liberal and conservative, likewise would attract large crowds of young people, especially when conducted on or near a college campus.

The purpose of all of these activities is to establish contact between young dropouts and the church and to begin the process of influence and dialogue. Traditional "come to us" strategies and normal visitation will not reach many dropouts because dropouts will not come to the church under normal circumstances and will not be responsive to visitation—except when a prior contact has been made and a relationship has been established.

Scratching Where They Itch

In addition to capitalizing on the characteristics of young dropouts, it is possible to focus ministry efforts on the felt needs of young dropouts, some of which are quite acute.

One of the obvious concerns of several dropout groups is

the need for a satisfying family life. For non-Christian singles who are on their own, life usually is either great or depressing, and it may change from one to the other on a daily basis. On Saturday they may be at the local "fun club" watching the hard-body contest, drinking too much, and trying to pick up somebody, while on Sunday they may be hung over and alone. Sure, they can get the excitement going again with a few phone calls and a trip to the lake or the beach, but at times they long for the stability and love they may have had with their parents or thought they had with their "ex."

The church can be a surrogate family for singles by making sure that opportunities for friendship-building are firmly in place among its programs for youth and young adults. Programs, after all, are only the *vehicles* for learning, fellowship, and worship; they are not ends in themselves. The problem, of course, is how to attract young dropouts to the church groups that can provide these functions.

Attracting young single dropouts will not be easy, but an active, exciting singles ministry is a possible solution. If the image is not one of social misfits holding hands in a basement "rec center" and swaying to the strains of "Kum Ba Yah," young dropouts will respond to the invitations of Christian friends and co-workers, if only to see if there are any cute girls or guys. And they may come back because of the atmosphere of love, and because it may be easier to imagine a more stable relationship with one of the Christian single girls at the church than with the runner-up in the wet T-shirt contest whom they met the night before.

Among young dropouts there are a few religious "seekers" as well as many others who would simply like to develop a coherent explanation for the meaning of life. The secular world does not provide satisfying answers to what sociologists call "ultimate questions," and home-brewed religious solutions such as the "Sheilaism" developed by a woman in

Habits of the Heart eventually prove unsatisfying and uncompelling.[9] The church is uniquely able to provide answers to ultimate questions and to give an interpretation of life that has stood the test of time. Yet many churches are somewhat hesitant about claiming to have any answers at all. Young dropouts are not searching for relativistic solutions; they want something concrete. Even though they may not accept the church's answers when first confronted by them, some of this group will eventually be convinced—if not by the cogency of the answers themselves, then by the difference that the Christian faith seems to make in the lives of many who do believe.

Finally, some young dropouts are in need of counseling—especially the group that I have called Sidetracked Singles. Persons who are in the midst of despair may be willing to accept help from anyone—even the church. Again, the problem is how to get help to those who need it most. Pastors and laity with counseling skills can offer their services through social service agencies. Churches can also offer crisis counseling services of their own to community residents who are alcoholics, drug abusers, potential suicides, battered wives, codependent families, and the like. The emphasis always should be on meeting the need that caused the individual to ask for help; however, there also should be the message that even greater help is available from God and from a surrogate family of believers—if the individual wants it.

How Do *We* Need to Change?

The church is a traditionalistic institution. It changes slowly, and efforts to alter its structure, values, forms, or belief systems are met with great resistance. To a certain extent, this is good because much of that which is characteristic of Christian churches should not change.

Attempting to do so would only undermine the distinctively Christian character of the church or render valuable programs useless. On the other hand, much of what is traditional about the church is neither good nor bad; it is only traditional. The "smells and bells" make us feel comfortable because we grew up with them. However, it may come as a great surprise for many of us to learn that some of the things that we love about the church actually repel others.

Our denominations need traditionalistic churches, but we also need structures that allow non-traditionalistic Christians to feel comfortable and that are attractive to young dropouts. This does not mean that we should jettison that which is central to our faith. It does mean that we should distinguish between what is scriptural and what is cultural, and that we should not allow our prejudices related to the way we feel Christians should "do church" to preclude the development of worship forms that are more attractive to those who do not share our particular prejudices.

The church that may attract young dropouts is accepting, not condemning. It is more concerned with the substance of the Christian faith than with religious or denominational labels. It does not appear to be a front for either the Republican party or the Civil Liberties Union. It shows sensitivity to the concerns of dropouts and other community residents by asking these persons what they need from the church. It is exciting, not dull. It may include contemporary Christian music as well as traditional hymns. It provides programs, such as home cell groups, that encourage the development of close, caring, supportive relationships— rather than letting relationships happen by accident. It includes people who are unapologetic about their faith in God and who act as if that faith makes a difference in their lives. It offers answers from the Bible and provides an environment where people can explore how to apply biblical principles to daily life. It is willing to engage in dialogue about the answers it offers, rather than asking its adherents to accept the answers blindly.

If this does not sound like your church, can your church become more like this? If this does not sound like your denomination, can your denomination include churches like this? If you would like to be in a church like this, why don't you help your denomination start one—or at least encourage your leaders to do so?

VI

Dropout Prevention

Once youth reach their teens and early twenties, the ties that bind them to their parents in terms of authority and influence weaken and often break. No longer can parents dictate where their children go or whom they see. The desire for an independent identity may lead some youth to a conscious rejection of the values and life-styles that their parents hold dear.

Church affiliation is often a casualty in this process of maturation and increasing independence. In fact, the church may come to symbolize the heavy hand of parental authority. For this reason alone, many youth frequently reject the church. In interviews with young dropouts and Mental Members, the statements heard again and again were, "I stopped going to church when I left for college," and "I quit attending church when my parents stopped making me go."[1] When pressed, most young adults come up with a *real* reason for dropping out once they have the opportunity. But whatever the reason given, it is clear that the *opportunity* to leave is of primary importance.

The church can do little to change the basic nature of growing up in America. There will always be a substantial flow of teenagers out of the church—most of whom will return after the church no longer symbolizes parental domination. The problem that parents and church leaders face is how to keep the flow of teenagers out of the church to a minimum, and how to keep those who are disengaging from the church from rejecting the religion of their youth altogether—and thus from becoming *Nones.*

A substantial percentage of those who stop attending church while in their teens and twenties will return. However, the larger the flow to inactive status, the larger will be the number who remain outside the church throughout their lives as Mental Members and true dropouts.[2] Furthermore, true dropouts are the least likely of any group to return to the church later in life. Once they leave, true dropouts are very difficult to attract or even to engage in dialogue about the church. For this reason, preventing dropouts may be more important than the strategies for evangelizing the dropout population.

Leading by Example

Humans adopt patterns of behavior and learn values primarily by observing the actions and listening to the words of persons whom social scientists call "significant others."[3] The mother and father are undoubtedly the most important of these significant others, as well as close relatives and older siblings who are in the home. Later in childhood, peers, teachers, and other important adults may come to rival the parents in terms of influence.

Although stories abound about the "hell-raising" children of preachers, there are undoubtedly many more sons and daughters of preachers who have gone into the ministry than who have gone into the penitentiary. Religious parents generally rear children who are also *eventually* religious.

The majority of Christians point to their mother as the most important religious influence in their lives. Indeed, the religiosity of the mother does tend to predict the religious activity of the individual later in life. However, information from a 1988 national survey also suggests that the father is of equal or near equal importance in impacting religious behavior. According to the survey, the church attendance of the mother and father while the respondent was growing up is moderately correlated with the respondent's current church attendance and with overall levels of adult religiosity—as measured by several indicators. However, the religious background variable that best predicts current religiosity is not the church attendance of parents, nor Sunday school attendance, nor childhood church membership. It is whether or not one's family usually said grace or thanks to God before meals at home.[4]

Unfortunately, many Christian parents are failing to provide a clear religious example for their children. Families no longer say grace before meals. Parents no longer talk to their children about God or about other religious issues. In many parts of the United States, Sunday school for adults has "died on the vine."[5] It is seen as something for kids. What sort of lesson does this teach our children—that personal prayer and Bible study are childish activities that are not needed by adults? If nothing else, it suggests hypocrisy. Adults say that their faith and the church are important, but they can stand to attend only one service a week, they never read the Bible, and they don't even bother to pray before meals at home—much less in restaurants.

The erosion of adult Sunday school, personal Bible study, personal prayer, and the perceived importance of faith apparently has impacted mainline churches to a greater extent than conservative Protestant churches. This may help to explain the high rate of "denominational switching" among most mainline denominations, the proliferation of Mental Members, and the high proportion of dropouts.[6]

A recent study of Christian education conducted among five mainline denominations and the Southern Baptist

Convention (SBC) found that only 37 percent of mainline adults read the Bible by themselves at least once a week. In contrast, 73 percent of Southern Baptist adults read the Bible once a week or more.[7] Is it any surprise, then, that only 13 percent of mainline youth age thirteen to eighteen read the Bible once a week in comparison to 41 percent of SBC youth?[8]

Religious activity is being trivialized by adults in many churches (including some church staff), and our children are watching. Children hear what their teachers say in Sunday school classes, but they pay more attention to what their parents and other adults do. What sort of lessons are children learning in your home and in your church? Are they learning that prayer and Bible study are important, or that prayer and Bible study are optional for adults? Are they learning that a relationship with God is the most important thing in your life, or that you should think about God for only one hour a week—and not at all during the summer?

An important correlate of growth in "mature faith" among youth is whether or not they have talked about God recently with their mothers. What proportion of the parents in your church have talked to their children about God in the past month? It may seem to be a trivial statistic, but, in fact, it is very important.[9]

Peers also are important to the religious development of youth. Peers do exert an influence, but the question remains, What kind of an influence? If a child has close friends in the church with whom he or she can talk about spiritual matters, then the influence of peers will be a positive factor in the child's religious development. On the other hand, if a child has no close friends in the church, or if those friends he or she has in the church are not interested in God, then the influence of peers can pull the child away from the church.

This brings us to the next step—involvement in the church. Before a child can be influenced by the church, he or she must be involved in church activities.

The Impact of Involvement

As part of the interdenominational study of Christian education previously mentioned, I conducted on-site interviews in a church that rated very high in many areas of congregational strength. It was particularly strong, however, in the area of youth education. The youth had high levels of faith maturity, and both the youth and adults thought that the program for youth was wonderful. Yet when questioned about the presumably wonderful youth program, the minister of youth said that it wasn't anything special, but that they did have a lot of activities for youth.

What the youth minister described is not only "a lot of activities" but is also a church-related youth subculture. The program includes Sunday school, a youth choir, a Monday morning before-school prayer breakfast, pizza outings or bowling excursions after evening worship, trips on the church bus to all away high school football games, trips to the state youth evangelism conference, trips to Six Flags Over Georgia three times each summer, trips to Christian concerts, weekly home Bible studies, counseling sessions with the youth minister, and even evangelism activities. Once a month the youth visit unchurched high school friends or those who have not come to church in a while. Adults go along on these visits as drivers, but they are required to stay in the car while the youth witness about Christ to their friends. All of the youth have been trained in how to share their faith. This congregation has combined the usual church functions for youth with a home cell group, a Young Life club, Evangelism Explosion, and a full slate of wholesome but fun social activities. It is easily possible for a member of this youth group to spend nearly all of his or her social life with other youth from the church and to draw all—or nearly all—of his or her friends from the church.

This level of youth involvement in the church is certainly

atypical, but it gives some idea of how the church can have a great impact on the lives of youth. How many of the youth in the aforementioned church will see the church as irrelevant or unexciting? None. How many will have a clear sense of the warmth, care, and feeling of family that is possible in a church? How many will draw two or more of their best friends from the church? How many will talk to their friends about God in a given month? The answer to each question is all. These are the very factors that are related to faith maturity, commitment, and the expectation of remaining an active church member after age twenty-one—or even forty.[10]

The primary characteristics that separate young dropouts from those who remain in the church are 1) liberal values in the area of personal morality, 2) an active *secular* life-style, 3) a lack of religious belief, and 4) the perception that the church is irrelevant.[11] In order to slow the stream of dropouts, churches must be able to teach children Christian values, to show youth that it is possible to have a good time without engaging in immoral or illegal activities, to show both children and youth the reality of God, and to demonstrate the relevance of the church to their lives and to the world. In order for these things to happen, the church must be able to "supply the goods," and parents must ensure that they and their children are involved in the life of the church. Through involvement, children not only learn the values of the church, but they also feel a sense of caring and support from other children, youth, and adults. Such an environment cannot be irrelevant.

What are the values that are being taught in your church? Is there any difference between the values of your church and those of the secular culture? Are you reaching out to the children of unchurched persons in the community? Is the active involvement of youth even possible in your church? Are adults available and interested in the lives of children and youth? Is there a sense of warmth and acceptance in your church? The answers to these questions will determine whether your church is producing or preventing young dropouts.

Keeping Religion Relevant

Of all of the criticisms directed at the church by youth (and by many adult dropouts), perhaps the most frequently cited criticism is that the church is boring and irrelevant. This may confuse pastors and active church members because to them the church is inspiring and very meaningful. Such confusion may, in turn, cause pastors and denominational officials to lay primary blame for the defection of youth on the youth themselves. Although it is true that some youth will leave the church no matter how objectively exciting or meaningful it is, our concern should not be to blame those who have rejected the church, but to determine how *we* are part of the problem.

The boring aspect of the church can be remedied relatively easily if a church is willing to make some changes. The first step, of course, is to find out the extent of the problem. This involves asking active and inactive church members as well as unchurched members of the community what they like or dislike about your worship service. If a transfusion of life is needed, one way to obtain ideas is to attend an African-American church of any denomination, a Charismatic or Pentecostal church, a fast-growing independent church, or a church of your denomination that is known for its exciting worship. You may not like all that you see, but what you will see are services that are anything but boring. Can certain aspects of these worship experiences be "baptized" or "methodized" and incorporated into your worship services? If nothing else, the strategy of including a variety of interesting worship elements, each of relatively brief duration, can be copied from African-American churches.

Clearly, most Protestant (and Catholic) churches could use more "life" in their worship services. The trick is how to develop a worship experience that preserves the liturgy and reverence which many churches hold dear, but which adds an air of excitement and expectancy. In attempting to do this, a pastor or minister of music would be wise to make gradual changes and to include the best of the old along with the best of the new. This will provide something for everyone: youth, young adults, baby boomers, and more traditionalistic older adults.

Making the church relevant is even more difficult than making a dull church exciting. Yet it is relevance, in addition to caring support, that will keep members active.

The feeling among young adults that the church is irrelevant results from two factors, both of which may be operative in your church. First, many youth have come to hold values that are directly opposed to those of the church, and, as a result, they may consider the values of the church to be irrelevant—regardless of content. Second, youth may believe that the church does not offer any meaningful answers to ultimate questions and is therefore irrelevant in the area in which it presumably specializes.

The solution to the problem posed by both of these factors can be found in 1) positive examples on the part of parents, church staff, and other adults in the church, 2) heavy involvement on the part of children and youth in the life of the church, and most importantly, 3) a clear articulation of values and beliefs on the part of the church. This "simple" solution is an extremely difficult thing to pull off, of course, because it requires a complete reorientation on the part of most mainline and conservative churches.

The need for positive examples and active involvement is critical. Still, such things will not be of much use in preventing persons from dropping out unless the church has a compelling set of values and a meaningful interpretation of life to offer youth. The church must have answers, not more questions or a vaguely stated moral code which simply reiterates the "nicer" values of secular American culture.

It is somewhat easier for theologically conservative

churches to articulate a definitive set of beliefs, values, and answers to life's ultimate questions than it is for liberal mainline churches. But the primary issue is not liberalism or conservatism; it is the articulation of uniquely Christian answers to life's questions. If a church has no concrete answers to offer, then it really has become a social club with no apparent purpose.

In addition to these answers, the church—whether theologically liberal, moderate, or conservative—should promote particularly Christian values. Such values can guide members to adopt a life-style that is in keeping with their best interests, even though doing so may occasionally conflict with the life-styles and values of those around them. The difference in behavior, attitude, and understanding will be noticed and will draw many nonbelievers to Christians with the hope of finding meaning and love.

For Catholics and Conservative Protestants Only

The strategies that have been outlined in this chapter for dropout prevention should be useful to all Protestant and Catholic congregations in dealing with the four types of young dropouts. But Catholics and conservative Protestants often share a particular type of inflexibility that results in church dropouts in a different manner from mainline Protestant denominations. For this reason, additional guidelines can be suggested to slow the flow of dropouts from these Christian bodies.

The Catholic Church "creates" many dropouts through a combination of indoctrination, unyielding positions on peripheral moral issues, and an authority structure which sometimes can seem oppressive. Because of the Catholic Church's moral positions, many persons who are divorced, who marry non-Catholics, or who disagree with the church's positions on birth control or the role of women in the priesthood are driven away.[12] Others rebel against the authority structure and become militant in their opposition to any attempt to mold them or tell them what to do. At the same time, the Catholic Church has been very successful in promoting among its adherents the view that it is the only true expression of Christianity. Consequently, alienated Catholics have nowhere to go. They find it difficult to return to Catholicism, but they cannot seek a more suitable church. As a result, some of these very estranged Catholics reject a religious label altogether. Many retain an identity as Christians, but because of their bitterness they can no longer call themselves Catholics.[13]

For conservative Protestants, the problem of creating very estranged youth is not as severe, but it is, nevertheless, real. There is a fine line separating parental concern and oppression, and a similarly fine line separating clearly articulated values and moralism. Efforts to teach youth Christian values and love for the church can easily backfire in conservative churches. Potential young dropouts want answers, but they do not want the answers to be shoved down their throats. They also need a moral code for living, but they will reject authoritarian efforts to force compliance. Many youth will blindly obey, but these youth are not potential dropouts. Potential dropouts want to know *why*, and if a good reason is not forthcoming, they will reject the rule as irrelevant. Youth of this type are easily driven away from their families, from the church, and from religion in general.

The key to preventing the creation of very estranged youth for both Catholics and conservative Protestants is to stress morality without being moralistic and to exercise parental authority without being authoritarian. Conservative pastors and Catholic priests should operate in the same manner with their congregations.

101

VII

Older Dropouts and Second Generation Nones

There is a small proportion of middle-aged and older Americans—including persons in their seventies and older—who reject a religious label altogether. Like young dropouts, they say "I am nothing" when confronted with the question of their religious preference. Unlike young dropouts, however, older dropouts are many years removed from "youthful rebellion" and apparently have left the church for reasons other than extreme moral liberalism or secular life-styles. Neither do many older dropouts fit the mold of the "town atheist." The question is Why did they leave the church when they share so many social characteristics with active church members? This is the issue addressed in the first half of this chapter.

Another group of *Nones* are not dropouts at all. They are persons whom I call Second Generation Nones. The majority of this group had parents who were *Nones,* and all indicated that they had "no religion" when they were growing up. Even though this group may seem to be beyond the scope of this book, by including Second Generation Nones I will have described all of those who hold no religious identity.

With the expansion of the dropout population among young adults in their childbearing years, we can expect the population of those reared outside the church (Second

Generation Nones) to expand. This group should be understood so that intelligent efforts can be made to reach the entire range of *Nones*—from young dropouts to Irreligious Traditionalists and Second Generation Nones.

Irreligious Traditionalists

The typical image of the older dropout might be that of the urban intellectual who has rejected the church and religion on rational grounds. Another popular image might be that of the "town atheist" who has foiled the attempts of many ministers to convert them. A less probable image of the older dropout, but one that has been suggested in literature on this topic, is that of the alienated factory worker who has come to see the church as "indifferent or antagonistic to working-class issues."[1]

It is probable that some examples of each type of older dropout do exist in American society, although their numbers are not likely to be very large. For instance, in his search for the unchurched, J. Russell Hale failed to find any urban intellectual atheists, nor did he locate any good examples of the town atheist.[2] Furthermore, the possibility of discovering many alienated working-class *Nones* in the American context would seem to be very slim. Despite the anti-church rhetoric of some union leaders early in this century, the higher incidence of non-affiliation among lower-educated Americans prior to 1960 is more plausibly connected to the fact that lower-class Americans were less likely to join voluntary organizations of any kind. The church was not singled out by American workers.

Rather than being urban intellectuals, isolated rural dwellers, or alienated factory workers, older dropouts in the United States form a cluster that has been labeled Irreligious Traditionalists.[3] This group contains persons who, surprisingly enough, have many of the social characteristics that usually are associated with church affiliation rather than apostasy. The Irreligious Traditionalist is older, married (or widowed), and politically as well as socially conservative. This group of dropouts also is *less urban* than most other dropouts, *less happy* than any other group (except for Sidetracked Singles), least likely to be unemployed or to be dissatisfied with their financial situation, and least likely to think that the lot of the average "man" is getting worse. They are also more likely to be female and to live in western states than are other dropouts. Some are likely to be widows or older couples who have moved to retirement communities in the West and have left social support groups behind.

Irreligious Traditionalists create an image of an older, politically conservative, economically productive family-oriented individual who holds social values very similar to those taught in the church.[4] So why have these persons rejected the church so completely? They have not done so because of youthful rebellion, unless they rebelled years ago and have not returned. Neither have they rejected the church because of value or life-style conflicts. They do not hold countercultural values, and few go to bars or get drunk with any regularity. On the other hand, as their name suggests, these dropouts tend to be irreligious. They are least likely of any dropout group to believe in an afterlife. Sixty-three percent of Irreligious Traditionalists say that they do not believe in life after death in comparison to 54 percent of the group of dropouts next highest in this form of unbelief (Sidetracked Singles) and to only 18 percent of those who retain a religious identity.[5] So it would seem that this group of dropouts is composed largely of unbelievers who reject a religious label out of consistency with their irreligious views.

Not all members of this group are atheists in the strictest sense, but nearly all are agnostics. As one woman said, "The truth is, right now, I truly don't know if I believe or don't believe. I do know one thing—just don't get up there and preach at me or quote the Bible."[6]

The reasons that Irreligious Traditionalists have rejected a religious faith are somewhat difficult to determine without additional information about their lives prior to the decision to drop out. We do know that an unusually large proportion of this group moved to a different state and thus were uprooted from the religious environment in which they were raised. We also know that a very high proportion now live in the West. As has been shown in earlier research, moving to a different city or state frees an individual from previous social constraints and frequently facilitates a conversion, a switch to another denomination, or a decision to drop out of the church altogether.[7] Also, residence in the West is associated with lower levels of religiosity.[8] It is, in fact, more "normal" to be a *None* in the West than in any other region of the United States.

When considered together, these factors suggest that a large number of Irreligious Traditionalists left behind their religious roots and found themselves in an environment in which a religious identity was deemed unnecessary. Some may once have been Mental Members who eventually decided to be honest and to drop the last vestige of the religion of their youth. Others may have been "free-thinkers" who questioned the beliefs of their church and came into conflict with church leaders, or who simply felt rejected. Still others may have been the young dropouts of an earlier era when the primary reason for leaving the church was rebellion against parental authority rather than conflict over values and life-styles.

It is also interesting to note that members of this group apparently keep their religious views somewhat compartmentalized. For instance, despite the fact that many Irreligious Traditionalists are atheists or agnostics, a majority of them (56 percent) would not approve of someone who was against the church and religion teaching in a college or university.[9] This odd position implies that many Irreligious Traditionalists do not believe that *people like themselves* should be allowed to teach and to spread their attitudes among impressionable college students. This group also has the highest proportion of any dropout group who disapprove of the Supreme Court's ban on prayer in school. So in the battle between their social conservatism and their irreligiosity, conservatism wins out—a fact which underscores our impression that many dropouts are more non-religious than anti-religious. Religion is not something they think about very much, nor does it impact their lives on a daily basis.

Reaching this group is likely to be a challenge. Even though they are similar to active church members in many ways, the lack of a common ground in religious belief creates a barrier that will be difficult to overcome. Returning to the church would be a major change in behavior for members of this group, but because many of them have experienced major transitions in life and are beginning to confront their own mortality, at least some may be willing to reconsider the church.

Second Generation Nones

Second Generation Nones were reared in irreligious families. Eighty-six percent of their fathers and 80 percent of their mothers either never attended church or attended church less than once a year. In comparison, only 42 percent of the fathers and 20 percent of the mothers of dropouts never attended church or attended less than once a year. Second Generation Nones were not exposed to the church as children, and they also lacked the example of religious behavior in the home—such as saying grace before meals, reading the Bible, and personal prayer.[10] With such a background, is it any wonder that the members of this group have remained outside the church throughout their lives?[11]

Additional background characteristics which are shared by many Second Generation Nones include living in western states and growing up in households other than the traditional mother-father family. Western states have never experienced the kind of spiritual "great awakening" that made the church such a dominant institution in the South and Midwest. For this reason, the West has retained something of a frontier spirit and has developed a unique religious flavor. There is no true religious norm in the West—there is only religious pluralism and a strong commitment to freedom of religious expression. A fairly large population of secularists who live in this environment have passed or are passing on to their children their irreligious values and lack of church identity.

In a similar fashion, divorce or separation negatively impacts the religious training of children because it apparently causes many parents (especially Catholics) either to drop out of the church or to become Mental Members. This prevents the children from having much exposure to the church. Some of those who are reared in this manner remain outside the church into adulthood.

Current Social Characteristics

Those who were reared as *Nones* and who remain *Nones* as adults—the Second Generation Nones—share many behavioral and attitudinal characteristics with dropouts. But there are some differences. Second Generation Nones are even more likely to be political independents than are dropouts. They are more liberal than dropouts on most civil liberty issues, but they are somewhat less liberal in their attitudes toward so-called new morality issues such as marijuana use, premarital sex, abortion, and homosexuality. They remain, however, much more liberal, on average, in all of these areas than the general population.[12] In addition, Second Generation Nones go to bars or taverns more often than dropouts (or anyone else), and they are more unhappy than dropouts on the whole, although not nearly to the extreme of Sidetracked Singles. Some also are "couch potatoes"—they read newspapers less frequently than dropouts and watch much more television, on average.[13]

Other characteristics point to the possible existence of several groups of Second Generation Nones. They typically are either very urban or very rural. Approximately half have never married, and half are currently married (and still living together). They generally come from *either* poorer or wealthier backgrounds than most Americans (relatively few are in the middle). They tend to score either low or high on a word comprehension test. Finally, although most are young (57 percent are less than thirty-two years old), the rest are spread out rather evenly among older age categories.[14]

These characteristics suggest the existence of a group of less educated, rural, low-income social isolates who were reared in families that lost contact with the church long ago. Another likely group is composed of liberal, well-educated young singles who were reared in secular families and adopted their values. A third possible group can best be described as Second Generation Estranged—those who inherited a mistrust of the church, but not for the personal expression of religion. This latter group holds no church identity, but they believe in God, they pray regularly, and they may even read the Bible from time to time. Finally, there appears to be a small group of true atheists and agnostics in American society.

Current Religious Characteristics

As a group, Second Generation Nones are somewhat less religious in all areas than are the dropouts. A smaller proportion believe in God or an afterlife, a smaller proportion pray or read the Bible, and a smaller proportion say that they are close to God.[15] True atheists are rare in this society, but it is clear that some exist—and many of those who do are Second Generation Nones. When asked about their views of God, Second Generation Nones might respond, "Belief in a personal God is just not rational," or "We are said to be made by God. Nobody else made us. Who gave us our minds or the idea of God? They say, 'God.' But what or who is God? Nobody can tell you that."[16]

However, rather than being atheists, most Second Generation Nones are agnostics or hold a vaguely formed belief that "something" is out there which religions call God. Some say that they simply never think religious thoughts or are not bothered by their lack of satisfying answers to ultimate questions. Others, and perhaps the majority, do think religious thoughts from time to time and wonder about the meaning of life (and death). Yet they do not view the church as a possible source of truth. The church, in their view, gives human answers to divine questions.

Since only 11 percent of Second Generation Nones never pray to God and *less than half* say that they are not close to God or that God does not exist, these *Nones* should not be considered unreachable by the church.[17] Although most *Nones* will be very resistant to the gospel, enough common ground exists with at least some Second Generation Nones to start dialoguing and to begin dispelling the widely held view among all *Nones* that "churches aren't too good for people."[18]

VIII

To Reach the Unreachable . . .

Are efforts to reach Irreligious Traditionalists and Second Generation Nones the evangelistic equivalent of Don Quixote tilting at windmills? Are both essentially futile tasks which accomplish nothing other than to cause people to doubt our sanity? If we plan to stand on a street corner and preach to those rushing past, then the answer is yes. We will accomplish nothing and most people (including other Christians) will think we are crazy. If, however, we plan to use sensible strategies, based on the characteristics of *Nones*, then our efforts may be anything but futile.

The primary goal of any evangelistic effort is to see men, women, and children come to a saving knowledge of Christ. Yet we should realize that reaching this goal is not within our power. We cannot cause anyone to become a Christian, and we certainly should not try to coerce people into making "decisions for Christ." All we can do is ensure that the unchurched are confronted with a clear presentation of the gospel in a situation that allows them to seriously consider a relationship with Christ. The decision to respond is their own.

It is likely that few Irreligious Traditionalists and Second Generation Nones have been "evangelized" in this sense. Many have rejected a distorted image of Christianity. They have heard vacuous restatements of middle-class morality and emotional ranting about hellfire and damnation, but they have never been confronted with a clearly articulated message of the Good News. An even larger number, however, may have heard a clear statement of the gospel, but the "signal" did not get through because of interference. Conflicting values, a non-Christian life-style, prejudices toward Christians, a lack of trust, and many other factors have effectively blocked the message.

Reaching the "unreachable" requires that they hear, understand, and believe a clear message of the Good News of Christ. Having a clear message to offer and even proclaiming this message are not enough. For the message to be heard and understood, a relationship usually is required so that the unchurched will listen to our words and seriously consider the message that we bring. Whether or not they accept the message is up to them.

Reducing the Supply of Irreligious Traditionalists

The population of *Nones* is in a constant state of flux. Its ranks are swelled by large numbers of young dropouts who leave the church as soon as they leave home for college—or for good. Its ranks are reduced when those reared outside the church are converted, or when young dropouts "drop back in." This process of shifting and sorting primarily involves the young, but in the end it produces a stable group of *Nones* who settle into a life-style that excludes the church. This aptly describes the experience of Irreligious Traditionalists.

Most Irreligious Traditionalists left the church prior to the cultural upheavals of the late 1960s and early 1970s. Thus, their reasons for leaving the church had little to do with the acceptance of "new morality values." There was no new morality to accept at that time; they dropped out for other reasons. In fact, they tend to share the conservative values held by most church-going Americans.[1]

It is too late to prevent the defection of Irreligious Traditionalists. They have already left the church. Yet with the "cooling of the counterculture"[2] and the restoration of the church as a valued institution in American society, it is likely that irreligion once again will rival rebellion and value conflict as a primary reason for leaving the church.

Strategies for preventing the production of new Irreligious Traditionalists include: 1) keeping track of members who move; 2) making concerted efforts to reactivate church members who rarely participate; 3) reaching new community residents (especially in the West); and 4) making sure that the message of the church is not only meaningful from a religious perspective but is also relevant to other areas of life.

Many Irreligious Traditionalists were once peripheral members who held unorthodox religious views. Upon moving, they lost their last connection with the church, and they eventually dropped a denominational label out of consistency with their lack of belief and noninvolvement in the church. The production of these dropouts might be reduced if Protestant churches made better efforts to "evangelize" their peripheral members and ensure that members who move are contacted by churches in their new communities. Mormons do a good job of keeping track of their members who move. Why can't mainline and conservative Protestant denominations do so as well? Some denominations are making an effort in this direction, whereas other denominations have no mechanism for tracking moving members.[3]

All churches should pursue a strategy of outreach and evangelism among new community residents. This is especially true in the West where irreligion is likely to be reinforced rather than reduced by the cultural setting. The "California life-style" is very appealing and often is adopted very quickly by persons from the East who move West. Many become "instant native Californians." Southerners who have never drunk alcoholic beverages start having wine with their meals. Midwesterners with sedentary life-styles take up biking, sailing, skiing, wind-surfing, or some other active sport. As they adopt various features of the "California life-style," Mental Members find that their unorthodox religious views and their image of the church as irrelevant are *normative* rather than deviant in this setting. The culture, therefore, acts to reinforce the irreligious tendencies of Mental Members. For this reason, churches in Western states must act quickly to contact new residents before the newcomers become so involved in secular life-styles that they become very resistant to outreach efforts of the church.

Finally, the religion that we preach and teach in our churches must be relevant to all of life. Most Americans tend to compartmentalize their faith, and potential Irreligious Traditionalists take this tendency to an extreme level. They hold social and religious beliefs that appear to be very contradictory. Churches must be able to show that the Christian belief system is valuable and relevant, not only in answering ultimate questions, but also in dealing with the problems of everyday existence.

Once dropouts have settled into stable lives as Irreligious Traditionalists, they will be very hard to bring back into the church. So hard, in fact, that strategies to reach this population must operate outside the church context—in the communities in which the dropouts live.

The first step in reaching Irreligious Traditionalists is in the development of relationships. Christians must cultivate friendships with neighbors and co-workers who have rejected the church. This can be done through individual initiative—rather than as part of a formal church program—as members are trained how to share their faith and are encouraged to expand their friendship webs. This process does not involve knocking on the doors of strangers; it requires only the cultivation of relationships among persons with whom church members already have contact.

Once a relationship (and trust) has been established, religious concerns, beliefs, and values can be discussed—if the Christian understands how to do so without offending the dropout friend. If interest is expressed, or if it develops over a period of months, then the next step is to involve the unchurched person in a group with Christians. This should be in the home setting rather than in a church. Outreach Bible studies, home cell groups, Christian fellowship groups, and other types of Christian house groups can be effective ways of bringing non-Christians into caring, supportive relationships with Christians in non-threatening environments.[4]

Another option for reaching Irreligious Traditionalists is to hold a class or to develop a special-interest group in a setting outside the church. The topic or project for either group should not be religious in nature, but the group should be led by Christians who use this as an opportunity to develop relationships with non-Christians who previously were outside their friendship webs. Classes can be held on a wide variety of topics: auto repair, painting, furniture refinishing, gardening, smocking, quilting, sewing, and so forth. Special-interest groups can include support groups for widows and single parents, discussion groups of various kinds, and hobby-related groups. Task-related groups may address community needs such as renovating low-income housing, helping to feed or clothe the homeless, registering new voters, fund raising for various causes, and so forth. The possibilities are endless.

An ulterior motive exists for all of these groups: developing relationships with non-Christians. Yet the Christian leader should not use the group as a way of drawing a captive audience in order to deliver an unexpected evangelistic message. If this happens, participants will feel exploited and may never return. The group should pursue its legitimate, non-religious purposes, but the leaders should use the relationships developed as a way to start the process of gently evangelizing their new friends.

Again, once an interest in Christianity or in "spiritual matters" is expressed, members of the group may be invited to another type of group. But the stated purpose of this new group should be religious rather than secular. It can be a religious discussion group for those who want only to talk about religious issues, or a home cell group for those who want to learn more about Christianity and the Bible.

Reaching Second Generation Nones

Second Generation Nones are not a homogeneous population. Although smaller in number than true dropouts, they are equally varied in their characteristics. Some Second Generation Nones will be just as resistant as dropouts to efforts of Christians to bring them into the church, whereas others may be more receptive than any of the dropouts or Mental Members. For instance, a substantial proportion of Second Generation Nones are not particularly irreligious in belief, nor are they truly antagonistic toward the church. They simply have had no contact with the church and view it as alien and somewhat foreboding.

I have never been in a masonic lodge, nor do I have any particular desire to enter one. I have seen their temples and have wondered about what goes on inside, but for me they remain mysterious institutions which hold no great attraction. The same is true for many Second Generation Nones in regard to the church. They may be a little curious, but not curious enough to attend on their own. After all, there probably are subtle rules of behavior which could be sources of embarrassment; they might be singled out as non-members and subjected to ham-handed efforts to get them to join; and, just maybe, the church that they picked might have strange rituals or one of those bombastic preachers like they have seen on cable television.

So Second Generation Nones stay outside the church, even

though they pray to God with some regularity and read religious books from time to time (anything from Billy Graham to Shirley MacLaine). They have a homegrown form of religion, which is rather ill-defined and somewhat unsatisfying but, nevertheless, able to provide some of the meaning and answers they need. Some of this group have inherited a certain mistrust of the church from parents who were Estranged Mental Members, but most view the church simply as an "unknown."

This group of Second Generation Nones is apt to be very responsive to the witness of the church—if the effort is made through relationships. In fact, one of the major ways in which *Nones* come into the church is through marriage. They marry Christians and begin to see something positive about the faith of their spouse and about his or her relationship with the church. Others may begin to attend church out of curiosity or for the sake of their children. Either way, they are easily reached by the church because their life-styles, attitudes, and basic religious beliefs do not serve as barriers. All that was lacking was a connection to the church, the realization that it had something positive to offer, and a vehicle for involvement.

I do not mean to suggest that an evangelistic strategy is for single Christians to marry non-Christians. The tendency of non-Christian spouses to "convert" is mentioned only to show that the best avenue for reaching this group is through existing relationships and through the development of new relationships. At least some of the *Nones* we meet will be very receptive to the witness of Christians. They need only to be approached and involved.

Many other Second Generation Nones are very similar to the groups of young liberal dropouts described in chapter 4. The only difference is that the Second Generation Nones learned most of their liberal values and secularistic behavior patterns from their parents. They inherited secularism rather than acquired it on their own.

Reaching this group will be very difficult, although not any more so than reaching young dropouts. Furthermore, the best strategies for evangelizing this sub-group of Second Generation Nones are very similar to those for reaching young dropouts outlined in chapter 5. First of all, churches should be aware of new residents in their communities, since moving to a new city or town is strongly correlated with conversion among those reared as *Nones*.[5] Persons living in apartments will be a major source of these mobile *Nones*, although gaining access to apartment complexes and establishing an effective outreach effort to residents is a very difficult task. Second, a singles ministry can be used as a vehicle to attract young liberal *Nones* to the church. And finally, seminars and debates can be used by churches and para-church groups to establish contact and dialogue with members of this resistant cluster.

Reaching former rural isolates who have moved to urban areas will not be quite as difficult. These persons may have grown up outside the church, but they tend to hold traditional values, to believe in God, and not to be antagonistic toward religion. In addition, research has shown that 80 percent of rural *Nones* who move to a new state, town, or county convert to some religious denomination.[6] This group of *Nones* is receptive to witnessing efforts. It is up to committed church members to establish relationships with these individuals and to welcome them into the fellowship of a caring congregation. Unlike Irreligious Traditionalists, this group may agree to attend a worship service at the invitation of a neighbor or co-worker. Efforts to develop a strong relationship with these individuals and to soft-peddle the church may be unnecessary.

On the other hand, if rural isolate *Nones* have not moved, reaching them will be very difficult, especially if the job is to be done by existing churches in the rural community. Such individuals may have developed deep prejudices against the churches in their area and may feel that they have been rejected and excluded by "those people." If this is the case, a new congregation may be required with the specific goal of reaching rural unchurched residents in the county. The pastor of the fledgling church may be welcomed into the homes of unchurched residents, if only to receive an earful of harsh words about the other churches in the area and their so-called Christian members. This initial contact may develop into a relationship which eventually will allow the pastor to present the gospel.

Finally, there is that elusive group of atheists and agnostics among the Second Generation Nones—persons who were reared in secular families, who hold irreligious beliefs, and who see no need for the church. Most of these individuals are not atheists in the purist sense. Some may believe in a supernatural power which they refuse to call God, whereas others are not bothered by religious thoughts. There might be a God in their opinion, but they have not given this possibility much thought, nor are they particularly concerned about the issue.

Reaching this group of *Nones* is likely to be very difficult. Because there are not many of these persons in the United States, churches are unlikely to have regular contact with them. The exception to this rule may be in college communities in which a long tradition of scholarly secularism exists. Cambridge and Amherst, Massachusetts, as well as Berkeley, California, might be good examples. There are many other such communities, no doubt, and their churches will be faced with the opportunity to reach atheists and agnostics much more frequently than churches elsewhere.

Atheistic and agnostic Second Generation Nones should be approached much like Irreligious Traditionalists. An outreach strategy calls for the prior formation of strong relationships with Christians. The next step is dialogue over the merits of Christianity and the validity of its answers.

Throughout the process, the positive example of committed Christians living distinctively different lives will serve to validate the arguments used in dialogue. The process may be time-consuming and converts will be few, but any other approach is futile.

Conclusion

Dropouts from the church—persons who have drifted away, who fled, or who feel they have been pushed out—are all around us, and their numbers are growing. This book is an effort to help concerned church leaders better understand what these people are like, why they have left the church, and some of what can be done to bring them back.

A necessary first step has been to understand why so many Americans have joined the ranks of the dropouts over the past twenty-five years. Misinformation abounds in this area. Although the first chapter of this book may not be the final word about what happened to church membership and participation during the 1960s, 1970s, and 1980s, it should help to dispel some of the myths that persist.

Much of the book has been devoted to "portraits" of various groups of unchurched Americans. First we met three types of Mental Members: the Estranged, the Indifferent, and the Nominals. These persons are on the periphery of our churches—not fully in, nor fully out—and their growth through the process of "partially dropping out" may be the primary reason for the membership declines experienced by mainline denominations in America.

Next we introduced four types of "true dropouts": Successful Swinging Singles, Sidetracked Singles, Young Settled Liberals, and Young Libertarians. All are young, all grew up as "something" from a religious perspective, and all now say that they are "nothing." They have completely rejected the church and its religious labels.

Finally, two additional groups of *Nones* were described in chapters 7 and 8: Irreligious Traditionalists and Second Generation Nones. The former are older, settled dropouts, whereas the latter were reared with no religion and claim no religious identity as adults.

It is hoped that these portraits have made it possible for you to develop mental images of various types of dropouts. Such images have more staying power than any list of characteristics. If you can also connect each of the types to a relative or friend, the staying power will be even greater. The chart on pages 124 and 125 may be helpful as you discuss the various dropout types with colleagues and church members.

These portraits are not meant only to illuminate our understanding of the dropouts we know or meet. They are meant to be used. Few churches are making successful inroads into the dropout population, and most churches have a very large "back door." As a result, real growth has been difficult for most congregations. Membership rolls may be increasing for some churches, but in most cases the growth comes primarily through transfers or through the baptism of members' children rather than through efforts to reach Mental Members or *Nones*.

It is not enough to decry the "lostness" of America or to preach evangelistic sermons. Strategies must be put into place to accomplish the necessary tasks. If church leaders are serious about reaching unchurched Americans in their midst, a number of very concrete steps must be taken.

1. Church leaders should determine the predominant types of unchurched persons in their communities (including those within their own membership). A community survey conducted by the pastor and a few church leaders is all that is required. The characteristics of Mental Members, dropouts, and Second Generation Nones described in this

book will help to develop a rough estimate of the unchurched population and its parameters. In addition, visits to lapsed members will give information about why they have drifted away or dropped out.

2. The pastor and a planning committee (if one exists) should determine which types of unchurched persons the church is best suited to reach. In other words, what can be done now, without a great deal of additional training or restructuring, and without causing conflict within the church? The goal of reaching these persons must be consistent with the purpose, identity, and role of the congregation.

3. Church leaders should determine who they *want* to reach—in addition to those who they might be able to reach easily. Resistant dropout groups will be more difficult to reach than Estranged Mental Members, for instance, but some churches may feel a pressing need to reach those who are in most need of the church rather than those who may be more responsive.

4. Leaders must determine the types of changes that are needed in order to reach specific types of dropouts and to better retain their own members.

5. A plan must be developed by the pastor and other church leaders that includes detailed strategies for reaching specific types of unchurched persons and the necessary changes in church structure. This plan should be based on the suggestions made in this book and in other resources for reaching dropouts and from the insights of the pastor and laity.

6. The plan must be articulated and sold to the laity as part of a new vision for the future or as part of the currently accepted purpose of the congregation. However, the plan should not be "dumped" on the laity in full-blown form. Members should be aware of where the church is going and why—throughout the process of planning.

7. The plan must be put into action. This will involve changes in worship, programming, training, promotion, and other areas. The strategy cannot become just another ministry of the church. It must be part of the identity and purpose of the congregation.

Suggestions have been given throughout this book for how to reach each type of Mental Member and dropout.

Additional suggestions have been made to help churches "slow the flow" of dropouts from their own membership rolls. These "handles" may not provide all that is necessary to reach dropouts and to close the "back door" of the church. They will, however, suggest ways that can be customized to fit your type of church, the strengths of your members, and your strategy for dealing with dropouts.

Finally, this book is about change and the need for change. A changing cultural setting, changing demographics, and changes in mainline churches have combined to produce an expansion of the dropout population and membership declines in most mainline denominations. "Things are bad, and they are going to get worse," according to William McKinney, well-known sociologist of religion. Although things may indeed get worse for liberal Protestantism—and even for conservative Protestant denominations—things do not have to get worse for your congregation.

Changes can be made and dropouts can be reached. Many churches across the United States are actually doing very well. Their problems are not those of institutional retrenchment, but of how to expand in order to take care of the hundreds whom they are reaching. To have this kind of success, American denominations and individual churches must take a hard look at what they are and how they "do church." Our traditions are holding us back. Even though it is not necessary for all churches to change drastically, more churches must be developed that are flexible enough to become organizations that can attract and assimilate the "unchurched Harrys" in our midst.

What can you do and what can your church do to reclaim dropouts you know, to reach out to those you don't know, and to "slow the flow" of persons going out the "back door" of your own congregation? Your answers to these questions may be the starting point for a transformation in the witness of your church.

Dropout Classification Table

General Type	Specific Type	Church Identity As a Child?	Present Church Identity?	Key Characteristics
Mental Member	Estranged	Most	Yes	Very negative toward the church. Substantial private expressions of religiosity, but no public religiosity.
	Indifferent	Most	Yes	Some private religiosity, but do not see themselves as religious and do not attend church. Liberal social values; lower levels of life satisfaction.
	Nominal	Most	Yes	No traditional religious beliefs or expressions of religious behavior. Liberal social values; lower levels of life satisfaction; many are males in high-status denominations.
True Dropouts	Successful Swinging Singles	Yes	No	Young; single; doing very well financially; fairly happy; active life-style; very liberal social values; irreligious beliefs. Many live in the West.

Group			Description
Singles	Yes	No	Young; single; not doing well financially; unhappy and pessimistic; very liberal social values; irreligious beliefs. Most are males.
Young Settled Liberals	Yes	No	Young; married; doing well financially; very positive outlook on life; liberal social values; irreligious beliefs.
Young Libertarians	Yes	No	Young; more libertarian than liberal; resist constraints; politically independent; not irreligious in belief; urban; socially active. Many are former Catholics; most are males.
Irreligious Traditionalists	Yes	No	Older (39 and over); conservative social values; married or widowed; very irreligious beliefs. Many are females, many have been geographically mobile, and many live in the West.
Second Generation Nones	No	No	Most are young. Liberal social values; irreligious family background. Many grew up in broken homes. Probably several distinct groups.

Second Generation Nones

Notes

Preface

1. It is somewhat unclear who first used the term *None* to label persons who lack a church identity. In the social science literature, perhaps the earliest study to use this term and to call for more research on this population was made by Glenn M. Vernon: "The Religious 'Nones': A Neglected Category," *Journal for the Scientific Study of Religion*, vol. 7 (1968), pp. 219-29. Articles by Wade Clark Roof and myself on denominational switching and dropping out have included the following (among others): "Denominational Switching in the Seventies: Going Beyond Stark and Glock," *Journal for the Scientific Study of Religion*, vol. 18 (1979), pp. 363-79; "Those Who Stay Religious 'Nones' and Those Who Don't: A Research Note," *Journal for the Scientific Study of Religion*, vol. 18 (1979), pp. 194-200.

2. C. Kirk Hadaway and Wade Clark Roof, "Apostasy in American Churches: Evidence From National Survey Data" in David Bromley, ed., *Falling From the Faith: Causes and Consequences of Religious Apostasy* (Newbury Park, Calif.: Sage, 1988), pp. 29-46.

3. C. Kirk Hadaway, "Identifying American Apostates: A Cluster Analysis," *Journal for the Scientific Study of Religion*, vol. 28 (1989), pp. 201-15.

1. Religious Belonging in America

1. The Gallup Organization, *Unchurched Americans 1988, Volume 2, Summary of Findings* (Princeton, N.J.: The Gallup Organization, 1988), p. 14.

2. Estimates are from the Research Division, Home Mission Board, Atlanta, Georgia. They are based on the assumption that a certain proportion of each denomination's adherents are "unsaved." These proportions are multiplied by the total number of adherents in each denomination, and the "unsaved" adherents are then added to the unchurched population to obtain the total estimated number of "unsaved" persons in the United States. Estimates of the proportion "saved" in each denomination are confidential and essentially are guesses based on theology, levels of religious commitment, and other factors.

3. James Allan Davis and Tom W. Smith, *General Social Surveys, 1972–1988* (Chicago: National Opinion Research Center, 1988, machine-readable data file). Estimate is based on 23,284 respondents.

4. Ibid. About 79 percent of Americans attend religious services at least once each year. At least 90 percent of these persons attend churches rather than non-Christian worship services.

5. Ibid.

6. Norval D. Glenn, "The Trend in 'No Religion' Responses to U.S. National Surveys, Late 1950s to Early 1980s," *Public Opinion Quarterly*, vol. 51 (1987), p. 309. See also Davis and Smith, *General Social Surveys, 1972–1988*.

7. Larry L. Rose and C. Kirk Hadaway, "Toward an Urban Awareness," in Larry L. Rose and C. Kirk Hadaway, eds., *The Urban Challenge* (Nashville: Broadman Press, 1982), p. 12. See also Rodney Stark and Roger Finke, "American Religion in 1776: A Statistical Portrait," *Sociological Analysis*, vol. 49 (1988), p. 42.

8. Stark and Finke, "American Religion in 1776," p. 49. Estimates of the number of church congregations in the Revolutionary era vary. The reported figure was derived from Charles O. Paullin, *Atlas of the Historical Geography of the United States* (Washington, D.C.: Carnegie Institution, 1932). This atlas contained the results of an exhaustive effort to identify and locate every church congregation in America in 1776. There were 668 Congregational churches, 497 Baptist, 588 Presbyterian, 495 Anglican or Episcopal, 150 Lutheran, 279 Reformed (Dutch and German), 310 Quaker, 65 Methodist, 56 Catholic, and 115 other Protestant churches, for a total of 3,223 Christian churches. Stark and Finke mistakenly used the figure of 3,228 for Protestants. This figure includes 56 Catholic and 5 Jewish congregations.

9. Winthrop Hudson, *American Protestantism* (Chicago: University of Chicago Press, 1961), pp. 95-96.

10. The Gallup Organization, *Religion in America 50 Years: 1935–1985* (Princeton: The Gallup Organization, 1985), p. 40. See also Roger Finke and Rodney Stark, "Turning Pews into People: Estimating 19th Century Church Membership," *Journal for the Scientific Study of Religion,* vol. 25 (1986), p. 189.

11. Davis and Smith, *General Social Surveys, 1972–1988.* Gallup poll estimates have been higher during the 1980s. The 1986 Gallup figure for church or synagogue membership was 69 percent.

12. Glenn, "Trend in 'No Religion' Responses," p. 297; Davis and Smith, *General Social Surveys, 1972–1988*; Jackson W. Carroll, Douglas W. Johnson, and Martin Marty, *Religion in America: 1950 to the Present* (New York: Harper and Row, 1979), p. 9; The Gallup Organization, *Religion in America,* p. 27.

13. Davis and Smith, *General Social Surveys, 1972–1988*; The Gallup Organization, *Unchurched Americans,* p. 50; Davis and Smith, *General Social Surveys, 1972–1989.*

14. Glenn, "Trend in 'No Religion' Responses," pp. 301-2.

15. Ibid.

16. Wade Clark Roof and William McKinney, "Denominational America and the New Religious Pluralism," *The Annals,* vol. 480 (1985), p. 29.

17. There has been no clear "liberal" or "conservative" trend in the 1980s. The proportion of Americans describing themselves as "liberal" has dropped greatly; but, in terms of many social values, the U.S. population has continued to become more "liberal." There are exceptions, however. For instance, the proportion of Americans who think capital punishment is needed has shown rather dramatic growth in recent years. The trend is mixed. If the nation has become more conservative, then it is surely what I call a "selective conservatism."

18. Data are from various yearly editions of the *Yearbook of American and Canadian Churches,* edited by Constant H. Jacquet (Nashville: Abingdon Press).

19. James Lowry, "Selected SBC Trends," *The Quarterly Review,* vol. 49, no. 3 (1989), p. 58.

20. Steven Tipton, *Getting Saved From the Sixties* (Berkeley: University of California Press, 1982), p. 29.

21. William D'Antonio, James Davidson, Dean Hoge, and Ruth Wallace, *American Catholic Laity in a Changing Church* (Kansas City: Sheed and Ward, 1989), p. 17.

22. See Dean R. Hoge, *Converts Dropouts Returnees* (Washington, D.C.: United States Catholic Conference, 1981), pp. 22-25. Also,

Dean R. Hoge, "Why Catholics Drop Out" in David Bromley, ed., *Falling From the Faith: Causes and Consequences of Religious Apostasy* (Newbury Park, Calif.: Sage, 1988), pp. 95-97.

23. The Gallup Organization, *Religion in America,* p. 42.

24. The Princeton Religion Research Center, *The Unchurched American: 10 Years Later* (Princeton: The Princeton Religion Research Center, 1988), p. 43.

25. Barbara Dolan, "Full House at Willow Creek," *Time* (March 6, 1989), p. 60.

26. After years of relative stability, the proportion of Americans who identify with mainline denominations began to drop in the 1980s. Data to support this conclusion are from Davis and Smith, *General Social Surveys, 1972–1988.*

2. Mental Members

1. This is based on an estimated 182.4 million adult Americans. Of this total, 59 percent are Protestants and 27 percent are Catholics.

2. This generalization and subsequent descriptions of Mental Members and how they differ from active church attenders are from Davis and Smith, *General Social Surveys, 1972–1988.*

3. Although the religious activity of both mother and father are important, the impact is additive to only a very small extent.

4. J. Russell Hale, *Who Are The Unchurched?* (Washington, D.C.: Glenmary Research Center, 1977), p. 46.

5. Princeton Religion Research Center, *The Unchurched American—10 Years Later,* p. 30.

6. Everett L. Perry, James H. Davis, Ruth T. Doyle, and John E. Dyble, "Toward a Typology of Unchurched Protestants," *Review of Religious Research,* vol. 21 (1980), p. 392.

7. Hale, *Who Are The Unchurched?,* p. 46.

8. Ibid., p. 47.

9. Ibid., p. 81.

10. Ibid., p. 67.

11. Perry, Davis, Doyle, and Dyble, "Unchurched Protestants," p. 390.

12. Ibid.

13. Hale, *Who Are The Unchurched?,* p. 65.

14. Ibid., p. 59.

15. Ibid.

16. Perry, Davis, Doyle, and Dyble, "Unchurched Protestants," pp. 389-90.

17. Ibid., pp. 390-92.

3. Reclaiming Mental Members (and How to Keep From Producing New Ones)

1. John Savage, *The Apathetic and Bored Church Member* (Pittsford, N.Y.: Lead Consultants, 1976), p. 60.

2. See D. James Kennedy, *Evangelism Explosion* (Wheaton, Ill.: Tyndale House, 1972), pp. 9, 13.

3. Hale, *Who Are The Unchurched?*, pp. 67-68.

4. Daniel V. A. Olson, "Church Friendships: Boon or Barrier to Church Growth?" (Paper presented at the 1986 annual meetings of the Religious Research Association, Washington, D.C.), p. 35.

5. Lyle Schaller, "Redundant Ties," *The Parish Paper*, vol. 17, no. 6 (1987), p. 2.

6. Kennedy, *Evangelism Explosion*, p. 14.

7. Princeton Religion Research Center, *The Unchurched American—10 Years Later*, p. 61.

8. Savage, *Apathetic Church Member*.

9. Search Institute, *Project Overview for the Effective Christian Education Project* (Minneapolis: Search Institute, 1989), part II, p. 90.

4. Young Dropouts

1. Davis and Smith, *General Social Surveys, 1972–1988*.

2. Ibid. The total is 14.6 million out of 182.4 million adult Americans. About 83 percent of *Nones* are dropouts.

3. Ibid.

4. Princeton Religion Research Center, *The Unchurched American—10 Years Later*, p. 43.

5. Glenn, "Trend in 'No Religion' Responses," pp. 297-99.

6. Davis and Smith, *General Social Surveys, 1972–1988*. For more information on the selection of these groups and statistical tables showing their characteristics, see Kirk Hadaway, "Identifying American Apostates: A Cluster Analysis," *Journal For the Scientific Study of Religion*, vol. 28 (1989), pp. 201-15.

7. Hale, *Who Are The Unchurched?*, p. 64.

8. Ibid., p. 85.

9. Hadaway, "Identifying American Apostates," p. 208.

10. Hale, *Who Are The Unchurched?*, p. 59.

11. Ibid.

12. Ibid., p. 86.
13. Ibid., p. 54.
14. Ibid., p. 46.
15. Ibid., p. 50.
16. Merlin B. Brinkerhoff and Kathryn L. Burke, "Disaffiliation: Some Notes on 'Falling From the Faith,' " *Sociological Analysis,* vol. 41 (1980), pp. 43-44.
17. Hale, *Who Are The Unchurched?*, p. 56.

5. Reclaiming Young Dropouts

1. 1988 Gallup data were given to the author in a phone conversation with a representative of the Gallup Organization.

2. In the United States, religious non-affiliation appears to be more closely tied to religious non-attendance than it does in Europe. The proportion of the population that attends church "practically never" is over twice as high in Great Britain than it is in the United States. Scandinavian countries have even higher levels of non-attendance. If non-attendance grows in the United States to a level similar to that of Great Britain, we can expect religious non-affiliation in the U.S. to double. See various issues of *Emerging Trends,* published by the Princeton Religion Research Center.

3. David A. Roozen, "Church Dropouts: Changing Patterns of Disengagement and Re-entry," *Review of Religious Research,* vol. 21 (1980), p. 441.

4. C. Kirk Hadaway and Wade Clark Roof, "Those Who Stay Religious 'Nones' and Those Who Don't: A Research Note," *Journal for the Scientific Study of Religion,* vol. 18 (1979), pp. 197-98. See also Davis and Smith, *General Social Surveys, 1972–1988.*

5. See Hadaway, "Identifying American Apostates," p. 209. Survey data from Davis and Smith, *General Social Surveys, 1972–1988* show that only 39 percent of dropouts have spouses who also are *Nones.*

6. Dean R. Hoge, *Converts Dropouts Returnees,* pp. 139-41.

7. Princeton Religion Research Center, *The Unchurched American—10 Years later,* p. 35.

8. See George Hunter, *The Contagious Congregation* (Nashville: Abingdon Press, 1979), pp. 91-92. Survey data from Davis and Smith, *General Social Surveys, 1972–1988* reveal that dropouts had less contact with the church as children, on average, than persons who are now active in the church.

9. Robert Bellah, Richard Madsen, William Sullivan, Ann Swidler, and Steven Tipton, *Habits of the Heart* (Berkeley: University of California Press, 1985), p. 221. The person identified as Sheila Larson essentially constructed her own religion, which she has named after herself. She has a set of moral codes and she believes in God, but her beliefs are part of a very private faith that is disconnected from the church.

6. Dropout Prevention

1. See Hoge, *Converts Dropouts Returnees,* pp. 85, 96-100; Roozen, "Church Dropouts," pp. 432, 439; and Hale, *Who Are The Unchurched?,* p. 55, 59, 77, 78.

2. See Roozen, "Church Dropouts," pp. 440-42 concerning return rates for those who drop out of active religious participation.

3. George H. Mead, *Mind, Self and Society* (Chicago: University of Chicago Press, 1934), pp. 151-64.

4. Search Institute, *Project Overview for the Effective Christian Education Project,* part II, pp. 84, 86. See also Davis and Smith, *General Social Surveys, 1972–1988.*

5. Dick Murray, *Strengthening the Adult Sunday School Class* (Nashville: Abingdon Press, 1981), pp. 44-45.

6. C. Kirk Hadaway, "Denominational Switching and Membership Growth: In Search of a Relationship," *Sociological Analysis,* vol. 39 (1978), p. 330; Roof and McKinney, *American Mainline Religion,* pp. 83-84, 167-68; Davis and Smith, *General Social Surveys, 1972–1988.* Also see chapter 1 of this book.

7. Search Institute, *Christian Education Project,* part II, p. 19.

8. Ibid.

9. Ibid., part I, p. 23.

10. Ibid., part II, p. 90.

11. Hadaway, "Identifying American Apostates," pp. 207-11, 214. See also Roozen, "Church Dropouts," pp. 438-39.

12. Hoge, "Why Catholics Drop Out," p. 95. See also Davis and Smith, *General Social Surveys, 1972–1988.*

13. Hale, *Who Are The Unchurched?,* p. 56. See also Hadaway, "Identifying American Apostates," p. 211.

7. Older Dropouts and Second Generation Nones

1. John G. Condran and Joseph B. Tamney, "Religious 'Nones': 1957–1982," *Sociological Analysis,* vol. 46 (1985), p. 420.

2. Nor did he locate any other true "village atheists," for that matter. See Hale, *Who Are The Unchurched?*, pp. 84-86.

3. Hadaway, "Identifying American Apostates," p. 212. See also Davis and Smith, *General Social Surveys, 1972–1988.*

4. Ibid.

5. Ibid.

6. Hale, *Who Are The Unchurched?*, p. 85.

7. C. Kirk Hadaway and Wade Clark Roof, "Religious 'Nones,' " pp. 197-98. See also Davis and Smith, *General Social Surveys, 1972–1988.*

8. Davis and Smith, *General Social Surveys, 1972–1988;* Princeton Religion Research Center, *The Unchurched American—Ten Years Later*, pp. 22, 29, 37, 39-40. Also, many other national social surveys.

9. Hadaway, "Identifying American Apostates," p. 212.

10. Davis and Smith, *General Social Surveys, 1972–1988.*

11. Data are from Davis and Smith, *General Social Surveys, 1972–1988.* Nearly all Second Generation Nones report that they have never switched their religious preferences. Thus, they did not grow up as *Nones,* later convert, and then drop out. They remained *Nones* from childhood to the present.

12. Ibid.

13. Ibid.

14. Ibid.

15. Ibid.

16. Hale, *Who Are The Unchurched?*, p. 84.

17. Davis and Smith, *General Social Surveys, 1972–1988.*

18. Hale, *Who Are The Unchurched?*, p. 82.

8. To Reach the Unreachable . . .

1. Hadaway, "Identifying American Apostates," p. 212.

2. Robert Wuthnow and Glen Mellinger, "Religious Defection on Campus," in Robert Wuthnow, ed., *Experimentation in American Religion* (Berkeley: University of California Press, 1978), p. 235.

3. The division of United Methodist Men at the General Board of

Discipleship of The United Methodist Church notifies pastors of approximately 30,000 moves by lay persons each year, for instance.

4. For further information on home cell groups, house churches, and other forms of Christian house groups see Kirk Hadaway, Stuart Wright, and Francis DuBose, *Home Cell Groups and House Churches* (Nashville: Broadman Press, 1987).

5. Hadaway and Roof, "Religious 'Nones,' " p. 198.

6. Ibid.